New Directions for
Higher Education

Betsy O. Barefoot
Jillian L. Kinzie
Co-editors

"Radical Academia"? Understanding the Climates for Campus Activists

Christopher J. Broadhurst
Georgianna L. Martin
Editors

Number 167 • Fall 2014
Jossey-Bass
San Francisco

"RADICAL ACADEMIA"? UNDERSTANDING THE CLIMATES FOR CAMPUS ACTIVISTS
Christopher J. Broadhurst and Georgianna L. Martin
New Directions for Higher Education, no. 167
Betsy O. Barefoot and Jillian L. Kinzie, Co-editors

Microfilm copies of issues and articles are available in 16mm and 35mm, as well as microfiche in 105mm, through University Microfilms Inc., 300 North Zeeb Road, Ann Arbor, MI 48106-1346.

NEW DIRECTIONS FOR HIGHER EDUCATION (ISSN 0271-0560, electronic ISSN 1536-0741) is part of The Jossey-Bass Higher and Adult Education Series and is published quarterly by Wiley Subscription Services, Inc., A Wiley Company, at Jossey-Bass, One Montgomery Street, Suite 1200, San Francisco, CA 94104-4594. Periodicals Postage Paid at San Francisco, California, and at additional mailing offices. POSTMASTER: Send address changes to New Directions for Higher Education, Jossey-Bass, One Montgomery Street, Suite 1200, San Francisco, CA 94104-4594.

New Directions for Higher Education is indexed in Current Index to Journals in Education (ERIC); Higher Education Abstracts.

Individual subscription rate (in USD): $89 per year US/Can/Mex, $113 rest of world; institutional subscription rate: $311 US, $351 Can/Mex, $385 rest of world. Single copy rate: $29. Electronic only–all regions: $89 individual, $311 institutional; Print & Electronic–US: $98 individual, $357 institutional; Print & Electronic–Canada/Mexico: $98 individual, $397 institutional; Print & Electronic–Rest of World: $122 individual, $431 institutional.

Editorial correspondence should be sent to the Co-editor, Betsy O. Barefoot, Gardner Institute, Box 72, Brevard, NC 28712.

Cover photograph © Digital Vision

www.josseybass.com

Contents

EDITORS' NOTES

There are a number of myths that cloud our understanding of campus activism in the 21st century. One of these myths centers on the perception that campus activists are "radicals." While such a characterization is not necessarily negative, fueled by the media's penchant for focusing on certain types of activists, one of the underlying assumptions of this depiction is that radical is synonymous with disruptive. It would be folly to argue that no campus activists in American history have engaged in disruptive activities, but those who did always represented only the smallest minority. The vast majority of campus activists have engaged in peaceful activities designed not to disrupt the "establishment," an overarching term to depict institutional inequities, but to change it.

Perhaps the most prevalent of these myths is the belief that students today, when compared with their predecessors in higher education (particularly those from the 1960s), are apathetic to engaging in activism. Such events as the Free Speech Movement of 1964, the building takeovers at Columbia University in 1968, and the national reactions to the Kent State shootings in 1970 have ingrained in our historical memory that those occurrences are reflective of campus activism and that current displays of student protests offer a pale comparison to the "high points" of demonstrations from the 1960s. This concept is wrong. Campuses have always experienced an ebb and flow of activism, with some points, such as the mid-1930s or late 1960s, representing apogees in student movements. The recent displays of student activism on American campuses signal a continued restlessness among the nation's collegiate youth over various issues. With the growing concerns among students over rising tuition costs, the enduring need to improve diversity and create welcoming campus climates for every group in higher education, the protracted War on Terror, and the economic recession, activists are expressing their views with a vigor comparable to most periods in American history. The rebirth of the Students for a Democratic Society (SDS) in 2006 illustrates not only the persistent presence of activism on campus, but the continual connections between the various student movements throughout the history of American higher education.

The purpose of this work is not only to help dispel these two myths but also to help those in higher education better understand the needs of campus activists. Even educational leaders in the 1960s, during what is considered the peak of student protests, had difficulty understanding and coping with campus activism. Campus administrators must be fully aware of the rights and responsibilities that student activists possess, as protesters

NEW DIRECTIONS FOR HIGHER EDUCATION, no. 167, Fall 2014 © 2014 Wiley Periodicals, Inc.
Published online in Wiley Online Library (wileyonlinelibrary.com) • DOI: 10.1002/he.20100

remain a vibrant subculture in American higher education. Those in higher education need to understand the best paths to not only allow student voice, but also help direct that voice toward peaceful and constructive expression. The recent brutality in dealing with the Occupy Wall Street Movement, or the unneeded pepper-spraying of student protesters at the University of California-Davis, shows that it is a lesson that some still must learn.

In Chapter 1, Christopher J. Broadhurst both frames the volume by providing an overview of the history of campus activism and shows how current activism often builds upon the tactics and ideals of previous movements. Chapters 2 and 3 examine two often-disregarded groups in campus activism: graduate students and faculty/staff. Too often assumptions about the nature of campus activism lead us to believe that undergraduates are the sole participants in protests. In Chapter 2, Heidi Whitford explores the growth of graduate student unions and how graduate student participation in campus activism impacted not only their own learning, but also that of the undergraduate students they taught and mentored. Adrianna Kezar and Dan Maxey continue this exploration in Chapter 3 by illustrating the ways both faculty and staff can work with students to support campus movements and, by doing so, create more robust forms of activism.

Chapters 4 and 5 detail the vast array of tactics employed by campus activists. By using the student antisweatshop movement as a context for contemporary campus mobilization, in Chapter 4, Cassie L. Barnhardt elaborates on various forms of collective action tactics and organizing strategies that today's students utilize to engage in campus activism. Penny A. Pasque and Juanita Gamez Vargas, in Chapter 5, focus on the comparatively newer method of performative activism and consider how student performances connect to social change.

In Chapter 6, J. Patrick Biddix links activism to civic learning and shows that campus protests can be considered indicators of a healthy civic learning environment. The concluding chapter, by Georgianna L. Martin, synthesizes the common themes of the volume and argues that campus activists are an integral part of the higher education landscape.

Christopher J. Broadhurst
Georgianna L. Martin
Editors

CHRISTOPHER J. BROADHURST is an assistant professor of higher education at the University of New Orleans.

GEORGIANNA L. MARTIN is an assistant professor of higher education and student affairs administration at the University of Southern Mississippi. She also serves as codirector of the Research Initiative on Social Justice in Education (RISE).

1

This chapter frames campus activism by introducing the historical movements that have been important for higher education since the 18th century to the present and exploring the connections and shared characteristics among these various movements.

Campus Activism in the 21st Century: A Historical Framing

Christopher J. Broadhurst

The expression of student voice, both on and off campus, has a long tradition throughout the history of American higher education. The nature of colleges and universities fosters such expression, and American colleges and universities, in particular, provide environments suited for student activism. College life often allows much free time that can be devoted to engaging in the social life of campus. For those with a greater social consciousness, such time can be used for political activities as well. Additionally, higher education promotes an active intellectual culture and, ideally, values independent thought. Universities even encourage extra-curricular activities by providing funds and space for student organizations. Not only do students often have a common bond of being of similar age, since everyone is on campus at one time or another, higher education eases communication between students. When students do communicate with each other, the growing diversity of campus enrollments helps introduce students to varying viewpoints (Altbach, 1989; Astin, Astin, Bayer, & Bisconti, 1975; Heineman, 1993). Furthermore, as students are on campus for only a finite period, it is sometimes harder to maintain movement momentum. Student leaders are only on campus for relatively short times, which often means students fight for quicker changes that allow them to reap more immediate benefits (Altbach, 1989).

The unique nature of campuses has helped spawn a variety of movements throughout the history of American higher education. This chapter explores the development of student activism on American campuses from the colonial period through the early 21st century. The campus protests of each period, while unique, often represent a continuation from earlier eras. Activists are often unaware of such connections, but strong protest

New Directions for Higher Education, no. 167, Fall 2014 © 2014 Wiley Periodicals, Inc.
Published online in Wiley Online Library (wileyonlinelibrary.com) • DOI: 10.1002/he.20101

tradition in American higher education exists in the very causes students fight for and the tactics used to achieve their goals.

Early Campus Activism: The Colonial Period and 19th Century

As the colonial colleges developed in the 17th and 18th centuries, campus administrators were sometimes forced to contend with students' rebellions against restrictive doctrines of in loco parentis, the classical curriculum, and substandard food and lodging (Moore, 1976; Novak, 1977). Students found the campus regulations particularly stifling, with punishable offenses including lying, stealing, keeping distilled liquor, entertaining nonstudents in their rooms, missing prayers or worship services, drinking, playing cards, going to taverns, playing pool, dancing, swearing, and associating with "lewd" women (Burton, 2007). A pattern also emerged among student rebels that would characterize student activism even up to the late 20th century: Often the more affluent students revolted as those from poorer backgrounds seemed more appreciative of their educational opportunities (Novak, 1977). Besides demonstrating against local campus doctrines, reactions to national issues could be found at colonial colleges as well, with students boycotting British goods and burning effigies of pro-British leaders in the colonies as part of the protests prior to the Revolutionary War (Rudy, 1996).

College students too were swept up in the revolutionary spirit that pervaded American society after the war, as campus demonstrations grew in size and scope during the late 18th and 19th centuries. Princeton alone witnessed six student rebellions between 1800 and 1830 (Rudolph, 1990). Although students fought for greater control over the curriculum and against what they perceived as poor faculty, the most frequent attacks were levied against what were viewed as disciplinary injustices by the administration or unpopular campus doctrines. Often some minor incident would spark a student revolt that was actually more reflective of an undercurrent of dissatisfaction with the administrators or faculty. In 1800, campuses such as Brown University, Harvard University, The College of William and Mary, and Princeton University endured student riots following such incidents as the suspension of students for loudly scraping their feet during morning prayers. While the revolts did not lead to changes in college rules, they were sometimes successful in reinstating the offending students. Violence often accompanied student riots during the 19th century and threats of bodily harm to faculty and administrators were not uncommon. In response to student revolts, administrators would enact stricter rules, expel the rebelling students, and disperse their names to their colleagues across the nation, essentially blacklisting them as troublemakers (Novak, 1977).

Campus Activism in the Early 20th Century

As the 20th century began, students slowly shifted the focus of their activism to issues outside of campus. Concerns over social reform were rising as more Americans began paying attention to the plight of the working class. Socialism itself was gaining ground as a political party, and student groups, such as the Intercollegiate Socialist Society (ISS), organized campuses in the struggle for social reform. By 1915, the ISS had over 1,300 members in 70 campus chapters. While the membership initially appears low, it should be noted that the entire U.S. undergraduate enrollment in 1912/1913 was only 400,000. Proportionately, the ISS could rival the better-known student groups of the 1960s (Altbach, 1974).

On American campuses, the ISS enacted educational programs that advocated socialism and social reform, particularly reform centered on improving conditions for the working class, to their fellow students. Some individual campus chapters became involved in such activities as organizing unions for student workers or fighting to keep military programs off campus. Antimilitary protests were not uncommon before World War I, as many students opposed military intrusion into campus life. Experiences in World War I showed the nation the horrors of war and led to a growing peace movement on American campuses in the 1920s. Campus issues were still important, as students demonstrated for ending censorship of campus newspapers, allowing women to smoke on campus, abolishing compulsory Reserve Officers' Training Corps (ROTC), and increasing student presence in college or university governance. Forecasting activists' desires for curricular reform in the 1960s and stemming from their belief that the growth of campuses had turned higher education into a business, students bemoaned the fact that the developing universities were negligent of their needs. Activists argued that the curriculum was not responsive to the desires of students and was not suited to study the needs of society (Altbach, 1974).

An outpouring of student activism began during the 1930s that exceeded, at least proportionately, the campus-based protests in the 1960s. Fueled by the Great Depression and the ascendency of fascism in Europe, the decade witnessed the growth of socialism and communism on campus. Old causes continued to be fought by student activists: abolition of the ROTC, censorship of student speech, strict collegiate regulations, and the threat of war. Advocates of the peace movement urged America to set an example to the world by disarming (Rudy, 1996). The sentiment began to spread to the nation's college campuses following the Student Congress Against War, a nationally attended convention for peace, held in Chicago in December 1932 (Altbach, 1974). Continuing this quest for peace, a group of Oxford students vowed in February 1933 that they would not fight for their country (Holden, 2008). The "Oxford Pledge" became popular on American campuses, and student groups held antiwar conferences throughout the decade, which witnessed students pledging not to fight in any war conducted by the American government. Students took part in peace strikes and purposely missed class to attend antiwar rallies. In April 1934, about 15,000 college students, primarily from campuses in the Northeast, walked out of classes to protest war (Holden, 2008). Nearly 18% of American college students participated in one strike alone in 1935 (Altbach, 1974).

Socialist and communist student groups continued to grow during the 1930s as well. With other smaller Marxist-influenced student organizations, the Student League for Industrial Democracy (SLID), formed from the ISS in 1932, fought for an array of causes that included workers' rights and the rising threat of military conflict. One of these groups, the National Student League, sponsored a national antiwar demonstration in which 25,000 students took part. In 1935, the SLID and the National Student League merged to form the American Student Union. Throughout the remainder of the decade, the American Student Union sponsored a number of demonstrations against war (Altbach, 1974).

Campus Activism in the 1940s and 1950s

Campus activism nearly disappeared during World War II, as victory in the global conflict was the priority for many Americans, including students. The patriotic fervor following Pearl Harbor essentially crippled the Peace Movement and reduced it to a core of some 1,000 energetic activists. Following the war and into the 1950s, the rising anticommunist sentiment contributed to preventing activism from returning to prewar levels. During the decade, students, as members of the silent generation born in the horrors of the Great Depression, World War II, and the Holocaust, leaned more toward conservatism and engaged in less activism. For example, although 33% of students opposed the Korean War, few expressed their disapproval by protesting (Altbach, 1974). Student expression, though, was not dead in the 1950s. Groups such as the Young Men's Christian Association (YMCA) and Young Women's Christian Association (YWCA) actively involved students in local community programs (Horowitz, 1986).

One form of activism that surged during the 1940s and 1950s was the battle for desegregation. Although great strides were taken during those decades, challenges to the concept of "separate but equal" began much earlier. Legal cases attacking the doctrine dictated by *Plessy v. Ferguson* in 1896 began as early as the 1930s. Students like Thomas Hocutt, Lucile Blufor, and Ada Lois Sipuel Fisher used the courts to protest the policy (Synnott, 2008; Wade, 2008). Spurred by the success of these early litigants against segregation, African-American students made amazing advances with their activism in the 1950s. Students not only continued to question the separate-but-equal doctrine, but also further tested the policy by arguing that they had an added undue financial burden as there were no equal regional facilities for African Americans, forcing those students to move away. More and more lawsuits flooded the courts, and African Americans increasingly gained access to higher education although many campuses staunchly resisted these legal advances, particularly in the Deep South. African-American student activists who were successful, however, faced an unwelcoming environment: separate dorm rooms, segregated lunch tables, and special sections of classrooms marked "colored" (Wallenstein, 2008).

Campus Activism in the 1960s

The great rise of student activism on the nation's campuses in the 1960s often reflected a growing dissatisfaction with American society and higher education in post–World War II America. During the period, rampant anticommunism abounded as the Soviet Union emerged from World War II as a rival to the United States. The ensuing Cold War between the world's two superpowers roused the fears of Americans, caused increased defense spending and a massive military build-up, and led to the expansion of federal involvement in higher education as the various governmental agencies pumped research funds into campuses on unprecedented levels (Geiger, 1993; Lucas, 2006).

This influx of federal funding to campuses, coupled with the arrival of baby boomers to campus, contributed to a great expansion of higher education following the war. Campus enrollments swelled from 3.6 million in 1960 to 8.5 million by 1970 (Lucas, 2006; Thelin, 2004). The expansion contributed to student complaints that campuses were becoming impersonal. With massive classes filling auditoriums, computerized registrations, and graduate assistants teaching more courses, undergraduates felt disconnected to their faculty. Students also had little input on university governance, the campus curriculum, or policies such as mandatory ROTC. More upsetting to students was the doctrine of *in loco parentis* that treated individuals who were adults like children. Strict campus rules governed contact between the sexes, enacted restrictive curfews, and regulated drinking. Students under 21 had their grades sent to their parents. Many campuses even had dress codes, policed the length of hair, and forbade facial hair (Anderson, 1996). Such conditions gave rise to the concept of student rights, and campus activists began holding demonstrations and rallies to have greater voice in their institutional decision making. Although the greatest example of the growing student rights movement was the Free Speech Movement (FSM) at the University of California, Berkeley that began in 1964, the sheer scale and media coverage of the FSM had a dramatic effect on the nation's campuses and helped popularize the idea that students should have a greater voice in campus governance. Following the FSM at Berkeley, other campuses experienced similar, if smaller, movements centered on student rights. A survey of students from 850 campuses during the 1964–1965 academic year found the dominant campus issue concerning students was the restrictive doctrine of *in loco parentis* (Anderson, 1996; Farrell, 1997). As students began challenging the policy, activists on each campus developed platforms for student rights that were remarkably similar. By the decade's end, the student rights movement had begun to secure the demise of *in loco parentis*.

While activists on each campus often fought for their student rights locally, national organizations emerged in the 1960s that not only took up the mantle for student rights, but also demonstrated for a collection of causes. Collectively termed the New Left, members of these groups, often dominated by White college students, drew inspiration from earlier socialist/communist student groups that predated the decade and focused on spreading the concept of participatory democracy (McMillian, 2003). Politically, the New Left confronted Cold War liberalism, a bipartisan effort by Democrats and moderate Republicans to thwart communism, both at home and abroad. Socially, the New Left also questioned the historic inequalities faced by those who were not White, male, heterosexual, and from a higher socioeconomic group (Gosse, 2005). Groups such as the Students for a Democratic Society (SDS), Student Peace Union (SPU), Student Nonviolent Coordinating Committee (SNCC), Southern Student Organizing Committee (SSOC), Young Americans for Freedom (YAF), and Youth International Party (Yippies) helped forge a sometimes unified cadre of campus activists. The New Left, which led demonstrations, such as the Vietnam Summer in 1967 (DeBenedetti & Chatfield, 1990), the Columbia University protests of 1968 (Slonecker, 2008), and the Days of Rage in Chicago in 1969 (Miller, 1983), made national news and evidenced the achievements of student activists in 1960s. New Left leaders, such as Tom Hayden (SDS), Stokely Carmichael (SNCC), and Abbie Hoffman (Yippies), became national celebrities. Never before had student activists held such a prominent place in American society.

The New Left, indeed most of the movements of the period, were influenced by the Civil Rights Movement. Continuing the efforts to desegregate education that had begun decades earlier, students in the 1960s intensified their resistance to both de facto and de jure racist policies that permeated American society. When on February 1, 1960, four students from North Carolina Agricultural and Technical State University (NC A&T) refused to leave a segregated Woolworth's lunch counter in Greensboro, North Carolina, the ensuing sit-ins that rapidly spread across the South provided a youthful surge to the Civil Rights Movement and invigorated a movement that by 1960 was losing steam (Chafe, 1980). Spurred by the success of the sit-ins, students took part in such activities as "freedom rides" to challenge segregated public transit in the South (Lawson, 1991), registering black voters in Mississippi (Bartley, 1995), and desegregating higher education. The glacial pace of change and acceptance for civil rights prompted some within the movement to abandon their previous approach to social change and adopt a more radical, and sometimes more violent, perspective. The ensuing Black Power movement built on a burgeoning sense of racial identity among African Americans. Drawing inspiration from this movement, student activists, sometimes through newly formed Black Student Unions (BSU), began issuing a variety of demands on campus: increased Black enrollment, open admissions for minorities, more hiring of Black faculty and staff, the creation of Black Studies programs, increased representation of Blacks in campus governance, better financial support for Blacks, and better working conditions for the nonacademic staff (a greater percentage of whom were African American; Van Deburg, 1992).

The success of African Americans encouraged other groups to seek their civil rights as well. The American Indian Movement (AIM) and National Indian Youth Council (NIYC) initiated efforts to improve conditions for Native Americans, including the expansion of educational opportunities (Gosse, 2005; Patterson, 1997). A Chicano Power Movement emerged in higher education, and a number of student organizations appeared on campuses, such as United Mexican-American Students (UMAS) and the Mexican-American Youth Organization (MAYO), which fought for improved campus climates, such as increasing Chicano enrollments, creating Chicano Studies programs, and eliminating racism toward Mexican Americans (Anderson, 1996; Gosse, 2005; Patterson, 1997). Asian-American student groups also sought improved conditions in both society and in higher education, including campus initiatives to create Asian-oriented studies programs and working in poor Asian-American communities to improve conditions there (Gosse, 2005).

As various minority groups were struggling for equality in the 1960s, both women and members of the lesbian, gay, bisexual, and transgendered (LGBT) community embarked on a quest to improve their rights. Inspired by the concepts of self-identity of the Black Power movement and coupled with the growth of feminism, female student activists confronted the rampant chauvinistic and patriarchal attitudes that existed in student organizations such as SNCC and the SDS. Women within the protest movements were often relegated to secretarial work. They were expected to cook and clean, and they suffered through inhospitable environments (Echols, 1989). Campus activists challenged discrimination in American higher education, such as discriminatory hiring policies or underfunding for female athletics, and advocated for Women's Studies programs and increased female enrollment (Davis, 1991). The Gay Power Movement fought discrimination within higher education, and lesbian and gay student organizations began to appear on campuses. The Student Homophile League (SHL), formed around gay identity, was created at Columbia University in 1967 (Beemyn, 2003) and, in the spring of 1971, Jack Baker, a gay rights activist, was elected student body president at the University of Minnesota (Farber, 1994; Gosse, 2005). By the end of that year, students had formed more than 175 gay student organizations on American campuses (Beemyn, 2003).

One of the most dominant issues on American campuses during the 1960s was the Vietnam War. Fueled by the expansion of the national media, horrific images of the war flooded American televisions on a nightly basis. For truly the first time in American history, war was brought home to the entire nation (Farber, 1994). Although a peace movement had existed for decades among students, Vietnam pushed it to new heights. What began as a core of only a few thousand ardent activists advocating for peace in 1960 transformed into a massive movement that could summon hundreds of thousands of supporters by the decade's end. At University of California, Berkeley in 1965, over a two-day period, 20,000 individuals took part in a teach-in on Vietnam. Between 20,000 and 25,000 student activists took part in the SDS March on Washington in April of 1965, making it the largest antiwar demonstration to date. Within five years, another protest in Washington summoned a staggering 500,000 activists, primarily college-aged youth, making it the largest single demonstration in American history. Students were not just protesting the war, but the draft, military recruiters and the ROTC on campus, and American military policy in general. The gradually growing restlessness with the war would reach new heights in May 1970 (DeBenedetti & Chatfield, 1990).

On May 4, 1970, 13 seconds on a small university in northern Ohio unleashed a flurry of unparalleled campus protests and produced a pivotal moment in American higher education. During that brief span of time, National Guardsmen opened fire on a crowd of protesters at Kent State University. Comprised primarily of students, the crowd was voicing their outrage at the American invasion of Cambodia. The barrage of 67 bullets that dispersed the crowd left nine injured and four dead. Images of protesters weeping over the bodies of their fallen comrades quickly flooded the media, and across the nation students' outrage over the shootings triggered the largest student protest in American history. Millions of students on over 1,000 campuses protested (Heineman, 2001). The accompanying violence, too, was unparalleled. Students and police fought at over 24 campuses. ROTC buildings were damaged at over 30 institutions, and authorities investigated nearly 200 arsons and bombings, half of those on America's campuses. Sixteen governors activated 35,000 National Guard troops to suppress the escalation of violence (Anderson, 1996; Heineman, 2001). Fifty-seven percent of campuses experienced significant negative impact on campus operations during the period, 21% experienced a shutdown of regular academic activities for at least one day, 14% witnessed strikes by student and faculty, 26 campuses shut down for one to two weeks, and 51 shut down for the remainder of the semester (Peterson & Bilorsky, 1971).

Protests in the Late 20th Century

Although traditional forms of protests did decline after May 1970, contrary to popular perception, students were far from apathetic. With even Yippie leader Jerry Rubin transforming into a Yuppie (Young Urban Professional) in the 1980s, students have been portrayed as driven by greed and self-interest in the decades following May 1970. Such a characterization is untrue. Students continued to engage in activism and display social concerns. Volunteerism increased in popularity, and causes such as helping the

New Directions for Higher Education • DOI: 10.1002/he

homeless, ending world hunger, and combating human rights violations became popular among students (Loeb, 1994; Rhoads, 1998). American foreign policy continued to draw the ire of student activists. The United States sometimes supported dictatorships with atrocious human rights policies. Students protested U.S. involvement in Central America and raised money to send medical supplies to the region. Protests against CIA campus recruitment, prevalent in the 1960s, continued in the 1980s. While most demonstrations were small, some brought out hundreds of students (Vellela, 1988). In April 1983, the Freeze, a campaign to halt the arms race between the Soviets and United States, sponsored a series of nationwide protests about the threat of nuclear war. That month, nearly 350 campuses took part as heightened concern over increased militaristic rhetoric between Moscow and Washington reemerged. Following the American military invasion of Grenada in late 1983, 20,000 students gathered in Washington to protest the invasion of the small Caribbean island (Howlett & Lieberman, 2008). During the Gulf War, student protests against the conflict sometimes reached the levels observed during Vietnam. Following President George H. W. Bush's November 1990 announcement that he was sending nearly 200,000 troops to the Gulf, a wave of activism struck American campuses. Demonstrations on some American campuses involved nearly 3,000 student participants, and on February 21, 1991, 250 campuses in 37 states conducted a coordinated national protest (Loeb, 1994).

The Divestment Movement emerged as the most publicized student protest during the 1980s. Building upon a movement that had begun in the 1960s, students attacked both the injustices of apartheid and higher education's de facto financial support of apartheid through investments in South Africa. Beginning in the mid-1980s, students escalated their push for divestment, with some campuses having hundreds of students take part in demonstrations. To further protest higher education's ties to South Africa, students built shanties that served as symbols of oppression in South Africa on a number of college and university campuses. The Divestment Movement proved extremely successful: 60% of campuses that experienced protests divested compared to only 3% of those with no protests (Martin, 2007).

Beginning in the 1990s, campus activism often centered on issues of promoting diversity, group identity, and multiculturalism. During the National Day of Action, on March 14, 1996, college students on the nation's campuses joined together to protest for a number of causes: increased access to education, the rights of immigrants, affirmative action, and better campus climates for students of color and the LBGT community. Recalling the methods of the 1960s, students held rallies, teach-ins, and marches. The event was followed by a National Week of Action, from March 27 to April 2. During that week, at Oregon State University alone, 1,800 students rallied against racism on campus; students at the University of New Mexico demonstrated to express their concerns that tuition hikes would hinder college access for low-income families (Rhoads, 1998).

Campus Activism in the 21st Century

As students engage in activism in the 21st century, they are building upon tactics and traditions that have existed throughout the history of American higher education. Although students are using new forms of technology, such as social media, to engage in activism that extends beyond traditional forms of protest (Biddix, 2010), they more commonly utilize such long-practiced tactics as marches, sit-ins, teach-ins, and street theater to further their agendas. For example, when the DREAM Act 5—five undocumented students attempting to bring attention to the importance of immigration reform—took part in a sit-in of Senator John McCain's office in 2010 (Corrunker, 2012), they replicated a form of protest first popularized in 1960. Each time students engage in performative forms of activism, detailed by Penny A. Pasque and Juanita Gamez Vargas in this volume, they are further cementing ties to methods of protest pioneered and perfected some 50 years earlier by the Yippies.

More than the tactics employed, students are often fighting for causes that mirror those existing since the colonial colleges first opened their doors. When students of color (Linder & Rodriguez, 2012), members of the lesbian, gay, bisexual, transgendered, and queer (LGBTQ) community (Renn, 2007), and females (Vaccaro, 2009) encounter hostile climates on their campuses and unite to change their environments, they are continuing battles that have existed for generations. At the turn of the 21st century, both the unionization of graduate students feeling exploited by their campuses (Julius & Gumport, 2003) and growth of the student antisweatshop movement (Bose, 2008) illustrate a concern for the plight of workers first promulgated by the socialist student groups a century earlier. Calls by University of California, Berkeley students, who were upset with the Israeli occupation of the West Bank and the Gaza Strip, for their campus to divest in two companies doing business in Israel (Hallward & Shaver, 2012) are similar to demands by students in the 1980s regarding apartheid. Views by activists that campus administrators are part of a greater power system in higher education that subjugates students (Ropers-Huilman, Carwile, & Barnett, 2005) eerily echoes sentiments made by Mario Savio during the FSM in 1964. Regardless of the time period, the tactics employed, or the causes fought for, one commonality exists among student activists: They are trying to change the world. That world might be as small as their campus or as large as humanity itself, but each student, each group, each movement, is moved in some way to better society.

References

Altbach, P. (1974). *Student politics in America: A historical analysis*. New York, NY: McGraw-Hill.

Altbach, P. (1989). Perspectives on student political activism. *Comparative Education*, 25(1), 97–110.

Anderson, T. (1996). *The movement and the sixties: Protest in America from Greensboro to Wounded Knee.* New York, NY: Oxford University Press.

Astin, A., Astin, H., Bayer, A., & Bisconti, A. (1975). *The power of protest.* San Francisco, CA: Jossey-Bass.

Bartley, N. (1995). *The New South, 1945–1980.* Baton Rouge: Louisiana State University Press.

Beemyn, B. (2003). The silence is broken: A history of the first lesbian, gay, and bisexual college student groups. *Journal of the History of Sexuality, 12*(2), 205–223.

Biddix, J. P. (2010). Technology uses in campus activism from 2000 to 2008: Implications for civic learning. *Journal of College Student Development, 51*(6), 679–693.

Bose, P. (2008). From agitation to institutionalization: The student anti-sweatshop movement in the new millennium. *Indiana Journal of Global Legal Studies, 15*(1), 213–240.

Burton, J. D. (2007). Collegiate living and Cambridge justice: Regulating the colonial Harvard student community in the eighteenth century. In H. S. Wechsler, L. F. Goodchild, & L. Eisenmann (Eds.), *The history of higher education, ASHE reader* (3rd ed., pp. 126–138). Boston, MA: Pearson.

Chafe, W. (1980). *Civilities and civil rights: Greensboro, North Carolina, and the Black struggle for freedom.* New York, NY: Oxford University Press.

Corrunker, L. (2012). "Coming out of the shadows": DREAM Act activism in the context of global anti-deportation activism. *Indiana Journal of Global Legal Studies, 19*(1), 143–168.

Davis, F. (1991). *Moving the mountain: The women's movement in America since 1960.* New York, NY: Simon & Schuster.

DeBenedetti, C., & Chatfield, C. (1990). *An American ordeal: The antiwar movement of the Vietnam Era.* Syracuse, NY: Syracuse University Press.

Echols, A. (1989). *Daring to be bad: Radical feminism in America, 1967–1975.* Minneapolis: University of Minnesota Press.

Farber, D. (1994). *The age of great dreams: America in the 1960s.* New York, NY: Hill and Wang.

Farrell, J. (1997). *The spirit of the sixties: Making postwar radicalism.* New York, NY: Routledge.

Geiger, R. (1993). *Research and relevant knowledge: The growth of American research universities since World War II.* New York, NY: Oxford University Press.

Gosse, V. (2005). *Rethinking the New Left: An interpretive history.* New York, NY: Palgrave McMillan.

Hallward, M. C., & Shaver, P. (2012). "War by other means" or nonviolent resistance? Examining the discourses surrounding Berkeley's divestment bill. *Peace & Change, 37*(3), 389–412.

Heineman, K. (1993). *Campus wars: The peace movement at American state universities in the Vietnam Era.* New York: New York University Press.

Heineman, K. (2001). *Put your bodies upon the wheels: Student revolt in the 1960s.* Chicago, IL: Ivan R. Dee.

Holden, C. (2008). "Patriotism does not mean stupidity": Student antiwar activism at UNC in the 1930s. *North Carolina Historical Review, 85*(1), 29–56.

Horowitz, H. (1986). The 1960s and the transformation of campus cultures. *History of Education Quarterly, 26*(1), 1–38.

Howlett, C., & Lieberman, R. (2008). *A history of the American peace movement from colonial times to the present.* Lewiston, NY: Edwin Mellen Press.

Julius, D. J., & Gumport, P. J. (2003). Graduate student unionization: Catalysts and consequences. *The Review of Higher Education, 26*(2), 187–216.

Lawson, S. (1991). *Running for freedom: Civil rights and Black politics in America since 1941.* Philadelphia, PA: Temple University Press.

Linder, C., & Rodriguez, K. L. (2012). Learning from the experiences of self-identified women of color activists. *Journal of College Student Development*, 53(3), 383–398.

Loeb, P. (1994). *Generation at the crossroads: Apathy and action on the American campus.* New Brunswick, NJ: Rutgers University Press.

Lucas, C. (2006). *American higher education: A history.* New York, NY: Palgrave Macmillan.

Martin, B. (2007). "Unsightly huts": Shanties and the divestment movement of the 1980s. *Peace and Change*, 32(3), 329–360.

McMillian, J. (2003). "You didn't have to be there": Revisiting the New Left consensus. In J. McMillian & P. Buhle (Eds.), *The New Left revisited* (pp. 1–11). Philadelphia, PA: Temple University Press.

Miller, F. (1983). The end of the SDS and the emergence of the Weathermen: Demise through success. In J. Freeman (Ed.), *Social movements of the sixties and seventies* (pp. 279–297). New York, NY: Longman.

Moore, K. (1976). Freedom and constraint in eighteenth century Harvard. *Journal of Higher Education*, 47(6), 649–659.

Novak, S. (1977). *The rights of youth: American colleges and student revolt, 1798–1815.* Cambridge, MA: Harvard University Press.

Patterson, J. (1997). *Grand expectations: The United States, 1945–1974.* New York, NY: Oxford University Press.

Peterson, R., & Bilorsky, J. (1971). *May 1970: The campus aftermath of Cambodia and Kent State.* Berkeley, CA: Carnegie Commission on Higher Education.

Renn, K. A. (2007). LGBT student leaders and queer activists: Identities of lesbian, gay, bisexual, transgender, and queer identified college student leaders and activists. *Journal of College Student Development*, 48(3), 311–330.

Rhoads, R. (1998). *Freedom's web: Student activism in the age of cultural diversity.* Baltimore, MD: John Hopkins University Press.

Ropers-Huilman, B., Carwile, L., & Barnett, K. (2005). Student activists' characterizations of administrators in higher education: Perceptions of power in "the system." *The Review of Higher Education*, 28(3), 295–312.

Rudolph, F. (1990). *The American college and university: A history.* Athens: University of Georgia Press.

Rudy, W. (1996). *The campus and nation in crisis: From the American Revolution to Vietnam.* London, UK: Associated University Presses.

Slonecker, B. (2008). The Columbia coalition: African Americans, new leftists, and counterculture at the Columbia University protest of 1968. *Journal of Social History*, 41(4), 967–996.

Synnott, M. (2008). African American women pioneers in desegregating higher education. In P. Wallenstein (Ed.), *Higher education and the Civil Rights Movement: White supremacy, Black southerners, and college campuses* (pp. 199–228). Gainesville: University Press of Florida.

Thelin, J. (2004). *A history of American higher education.* Baltimore, MD: John Hopkins University Press.

Vaccaro, A. (2009). Third wave feminist undergraduates: Transforming identities and redirecting activism in response to institutional sexism. *NASPA Journal About Women in Higher Education*, 2(1), 3–27.

Van Deburg, W. (1992). *New day in Babylon: The Black Power movement and American culture, 1965–1975.* Chicago, IL: University of Chicago Press.

Vellela, T. (1988). *New voices: Student activism in the '80s and '90s.* Boston, MA: South End Press.

Wade, M. (2008). Four who would: Constantine v. Southwestern Louisiana Institute (1954) and the desegregation of Louisiana's state colleges. In P. Wallenstein (Ed.),

Higher education and the Civil Rights movement: White supremacy, Black southerners, and college campuses (pp. 60–91). Gainesville: University Press of Florida.

Wallenstein, P. (2008). Black southerners and nonblack universities: The process of desegregating southern higher education. In P. Wallenstein (Ed.), *Higher education and the Civil Rights Movement: White supremacy, Black southerners, and college campuses* (pp. 17–59). Gainesville: University Press of Florida.

CHRISTOPHER J. BROADHURST *is an assistant professor of higher education at the University of New Orleans.*

2

Graduate student unionization efforts have made an indelible mark on the higher education milieu, as illustrated by the experiences of students who participated in this movement in recent years.

The Role of Graduate Student Unions in the Higher Education Landscape

Heidi Whitford

Between the 1990s and early 2000s and continuing to the present day, graduate student unions have become more prevalent across the higher education landscape, making their mark on the campus climate and organizational structure of universities. The strength of these groups has fluctuated over the years in relation to various factors such as laws governing organized labor, changing responsibilities and conditions of graduate student labor, and the shifting tides of graduate student financial support and the academic labor market. This chapter builds on prior research by examining the contemporary context of activists and, in particular, by exploring how the presence of unions affects the everyday lives, learning experiences, and mentoring relationships of graduate students. Through a qualitative case study approach, graduate student union activists provided in-depth data that permitted a multifaceted analysis of the intersection of their identities, roles, and power struggles. Their participation in campus activism had an impact not only on the learning of the graduate students themselves, but also on that of the undergraduate students they taught and mentored. Their participation in the unionizing movement also affected their academic careers and interactions with faculty and administrators. As an analysis of individual case studies juxtaposed with historical and recent research on graduate student labor and unions, this chapter provides a nuanced window into the contemporary context of graduate student union activism as seen through the perspective of active participants.

The Development of Graduate Student Unions

As Rhoades and Rhoads (2002) noted, the decade of the 1990s brought about a large increase in the unionization of graduate students, with the number of graduate student unions increasing from just five at the

NEW DIRECTIONS FOR HIGHER EDUCATION, no. 167, Fall 2014   © 2014 Wiley Periodicals, Inc.
Published online in Wiley Online Library (wileyonlinelibrary.com) • DOI: 10.1002/he.20102

beginning of the decade to as many as 40 at the end of the decade. Frequently, the formation of graduate student unions depended on student leaders collaborating with other already established unions, including faculty and adjunct unions (Wickens, 2008). In addition, the organizers often collaborated with larger labor unions outside the higher education setting. The leaders of labor unions throughout the United States offered their skills and support to many of the campus-based unions (Rhoades & Rhoads, 2002).

In Rhoades and Rhoads's (2002) study of the subjective reality of graduate student union participants, they investigated how graduate student union activities influenced the identity development of student union activists. Rhoades and Rhoads used theories of power structures and critical postmodern identity politics that framed an analysis of power, social relationships, and identity among the participants in the graduate student union movement. The authors identified class, cultural identity, and ideological proclivity as important factors in the identity formation of graduate student activists. The case studies illustrated in this chapter bring some of these factors into clearer view and further explore the complexities of graduate student activists' identities.

The National Labor Relations Board.   Rhoades and Rhoads (2002) found that the ability of groups to unionize legally was constrained by collective bargaining laws and statutes that vary from state to state and often change with legislative decisions and political trends. For example, until 2000, only graduate students at public universities were permitted to form unions under the rules of the National Labor Relations Board, the federal agency that governs unions in the United States. Graduate student employees, whether they were teaching or research assistants, were considered student apprentices, rather than employees. Flora (2007) also considered the question of the legal status of graduate assistants: Were they considered employees or students?

It was not until 2000 that the National Labor Relations Board ruled that graduate assistants at private universities could be included within the parameters of the National Labor Relations Act (National Labor Relations Board, n.d.). Thus, although the affected universities appealed the ruling and later successfully overturned it, the initial ruling opened a window of opportunity for other campus-based graduate student unions to form at both public and private universities (Rhoades & Rhoads, 2002). The case studies examined in this chapter took place at a private university that was not legally required to permit unionization by graduate students; thus, the legal environment further influenced the experiences the students described.

Graduate Student Unions and the Academic Labor Market. Dixon, Tope, and Dyke (2008) contributed to the research on graduate student unions by grounding it within the context of larger U.S. labor movements and the academic labor market. Using quantitative analysis methods, they defined which variables were likely to be conducive to successful student union mobilization efforts. In addition, they examined the activities of graduate student unions, including membership campaigns and demonstrations. They discussed the importance of historical context in the development of the movement toward graduate student unions, stating that changes in the academic labor market, such as the increasing use of adjuncts and non-tenure-track faculty, have led to increased motivation to join labor unions. Dixon et al. noted that graduate students at elite schools often were more likely to engage in union and protest activities, which points to resource mobilization theory: If students have enough resources, they are more likely to mobilize effectively.

Singh, Zinni, and MacLennan (2006) also approached the topic of student collective action from the perspective of graduate student unions. Citing the increasing numbers of union members among graduate assistants and faculty, the researchers argued that the domain of higher education might well become an area of strong union influence. Historical and descriptive in its approach, their study contained many legal details about the university policies and state laws that govern union membership and the legal right to collective bargaining, but relates the development of graduate student unions to the student activism that took place in the 1960s, particularly on the University of California, Berkeley campus.

Singh et al. (2006) argued that the growth and function of graduate student unions could be related to the shift of the university structure to a corporate, business-like model. This shift to a more corporate model affected the workload of graduate assistants: "The traditional model of the university, as we once knew it, is now replaced by one that runs itself as a business, seeking to make profits" (Singh et al., 2006, p. 67). Interestingly, the researchers argued that university administrators have opposed union organizing on campuses because of their view that universities are not like corporations, and therefore unions do not fit within the academic culture. While the research of Singh et al. (2006) did not analyze the political ideology and motivation behind the increase in unionization of graduate students, they indicated that such topics needed further research.

Although prior research has alluded to the increased corporatization of universities as a factor in the worsening labor conditions of graduate student assistants, few researchers make the link between these factors and the motivation of graduate students to join unions. One notable exception is the analysis of Bousquet and Nelson (2008), who described the linkages between academic labor markets, the corporatization of higher education, and the conditions that foster unionization efforts by graduate students.

As the prior research demonstrates, graduate student union activism takes place in a complex environment in which many factors come into play: Higher education finance, labor market conditions, the changing management structure of higher education, and student identity development are just a few of the issues that have grown in importance within the study of higher education. Moreover, it is important to note the process of learning that occurred with graduate students as they made the decision to organize a union to protect their rights as graduate student workers. This type of learning is vital since it is fueled by a passion to stand up to authorities for what the graduate students believed to be fair and just. In the case study examples provided herein, learning extended beyond the classroom and was part of a distinct transformation that occurred from such experiences.

Case Studies

For this chapter, the researcher drew individual cases from the graduate student union activists at a large, private university in an urban area of the United States. The cases represent three individuals who worked in various capacities as both graduate student assistants and as graduate student union activists. Note that in the descriptions, all names and identifying details have been changed and any similarity to actual people is purely coincidental.

The researcher used narrative research methods of extended, open-ended interviews that took place at the case study site (Riessman, 2008). The stories illuminate the everyday struggles and triumphs of the activists as they reflected on their work as students, teachers, and activists.

Background and Context.   The story of the graduate student union, as told by several of the study participants, also elicited recollections of the origins of the group and the various challenges, successes, and failures that the group experienced over the years since its inception. The graduate student union was formed in the late 1990s amid growing concerns among graduate students about the conditions of the academic labor market, but did not gain prominence until the mid-2000s when the union was faced with the challenge of the contract for graduate student workers being allowed to expire without renewal by the university administration.

About two years after forming a union, the graduate students persuaded the university administration to enter into negotiations for a contract. At that time, the university administration established a labor contract for graduate student employees, but this contract was allowed to expire after a few years. After it expired, the university declined to establish a new contract or enter into negotiations with the graduate student union. The contract had covered areas such as pay, working conditions, and health insurance.

The administration's decision to let the graduate student union's contract to expire followed the precedent of another university that decided to rescind permission to allow a graduate student labor union. This decision, according to the graduate student union website, was attributed in part to the antiunion stance of the Republican Party majority in the U.S. political arena at the time. The administration allowed the graduate student employee contract to expire, but even more troubling, the university did not allow the graduate student union to negotiate a new contract.

The contract expiration set in motion a series of events and conflicts between the graduate student union and the university administration. After this battle was lost with the administration, the graduate student workers continued to take part in union activities, although the graduate student union remained officially unrecognized by the university. Shortly thereafter, the graduate student union organized a strike of the graduate student workers. This strike, while ultimately not successful in forcing the administration to recognize the union's right to negotiate a contract, propelled the graduate student union activists into the media spotlight and made many students, faculty, and the academic community more aware of the circumstances faced by graduate student employees. Thus, the stage was set for the following three case studies, which illustrate the struggles of graduate student activists at this university during this time period.

Balancing Social Justice and Privilege.   Natalie, a doctoral student in the social sciences, began as an active member of the graduate student union. Her experience illustrated the painstaking balancing act of graduate student activists given their many roles; among these roles were student, instructor, social justice advocate, and researcher. Although her role in the union gradually waned, her basic academic, moral, and social philosophy remained strongly connected to the graduate student union's mission. She described her experience, and that of her fellow graduate student activists, as follows:

> There seemed to be a lot of students who were involved in projects outside of their classwork and their direct academic research. There were people who had been journalists, or full-time activists, or nonprofit workers before they went back to school. And all of that made me feel like this program was more connected to social justice work than a more traditional PhD program.

Natalie described her academic department as being both supportive and encouraging for students who wanted to devote themselves to socially progressive causes and beliefs, including such activities as volunteer work or community organizing. This supportive environment, according to Natalie, was what drew her to the department. Moreover, she observed that many of the other students in her program had similar interests in social justice and progressive politics.

Long before joining the graduate student union, Natalie cultivated a deeply held interest in social justice and community organizing. She worked for an organization that helped immigrant teens become politically active and learn community organizing skills. Each summer, Natalie worked with this organization to facilitate youth workshops covering areas such as leadership, political empowerment, and other strategic skills. The organization's purpose was to assist this group of youths who, according to Natalie, were often found at the margins of society because of their adolescent, minority, and immigrant status. These types of service activities, Natalie felt, had more of an impact on society than what she did with the graduate student union. However, she noted that being a graduate student made it easier to fit her service work within her life by providing her with time and resources.

Like other graduate student union activists who participated in this study, Natalie agreed that supporting the union in its efforts to negotiate with the university administration for a contract was a moral imperative. From the beginning of her program of study, Natalie joined forces with the graduate student union and began attending meetings and events. These meetings and events led up to the organization of the graduate student strike, which began as a response to the university administrators' decision to let the previous graduate student worker contract expire without renegotiations.

The strike, according to Natalie's description, had a profound impact on her during the academic year that it took place. It became a source of stress and anxiety as graduate students refused to perform their assigned teaching-assistant duties. Professors had to alter their syllabi in order to compensate for the missing graduate teaching assistants who normally would be grading assignments and exams and holding recitation sessions and office hours. Furthermore, Natalie reported that during the strike many professors held classes off campus in order to show their support for the striking graduate students. Even though the strike had a direct impact on teaching, Natalie discussed at length how the professors in her department were supportive of the strike.

As the strike wore on, however, Natalie continued to feel an increasing amount of stress and anxiety. Many of her fellow students lost their university positions and stipends as a result of going on strike, and she did not know when or if she and other students would experience the same fate. As graduate students, their main sources of income were the stipends and fellowships received from their positions as teaching or research assistants. Their livelihood was under possible threat from the university administration's response to the strike.

As the strike continued into another semester, Natalie began to question the effectiveness of the strategy. It became clear to her that morale was running low as the strike continued month after month, and graduate students were showing signs of fatigue as their level of stress increased. Despite the lengthy duration of the strike, the administration refused to change its position regarding a renegotiation of a graduate student worker contract, and the student activists finally decided to end the strike.

By the time the strike had ended in the spring semester, Natalie began to question the tactics and strategies of the graduate student union

New Directions for Higher Education • DOI: 10.1002/he

organizers. In some respects, she felt that she did not agree with many of these strategies. Dissident voices, such as hers, however, were not given much credence in the graduate student union meetings because the leaders felt it was more important to continue the strike as a united front for as long as possible, rather than pause to question their tactics.

Natalie's disillusionment with the graduate student union strike influenced her later reflections on the union's activities and caused her to question her own involvement. After the strike ended, she began to curtail her regular participation in union meetings and events. Although she continued to be a union member, she gradually withdrew from participating. This gave her the time and energy to engage more in the activist pursuits that were important to her. According to Natalie, "Students who get interested in issues around social justice, if they feel frustrated with campus politics they are going to go do work elsewhere." Thus, she began to pursue her interest in researching immigrants' working conditions and labor rights. In addition, she continued her work in organizing political empowerment workshops with immigrant youth.

As Natalie continued her work with progressive causes, she reflected on the position of relative privilege that she held as a graduate student at an elite university. She often thought about the possible contradictions between her privileged position as a graduate student and the immigrants with whom she worked who were often in marginal positions in society and faced conditions of poverty and discrimination. She observed that this contradiction between poverty and privilege even had an impact on the ability of people to engage in protests, demonstrations, or other organized acts of dissent or activism.

For example, Natalie observed that many undocumented immigrants could not advocate for themselves through public forms of protest for fear of deportation, arrest, or further discrimination. Furthermore, she observed that people who were very poor would be less able to engage in public forms of protest that might possibly end in arrest because they would have fewer resources to extricate themselves from the legal system. In these instances, Natalie reflected on the stark difference between the actions of the graduate student union members, a group characterized by relative privilege, and the actions of immigrants or undocumented workers who were fighting for their rights. For the above reasons, Natalie preferred working with marginalized groups rather than with the graduate student union. Her participation in the graduate student union strike helped her gain the clarity to discern her true purpose, which was to utilize her knowledge and skills in community organizing efforts to further empower others.

Creating Community Within Academia.   Tyler was a member of the graduate student union, but his active participation, in contrast to Natalie's, began after the strike had ended. Tyler's reflection on his participation was different from Natalie's as some of the negative emotions surrounding the strike had dissipated by the time Tyler became involved. Moreover, as Tyler discussed, the leadership had also changed as most of the previous leaders had graduated.

When Tyler arrived on campus as a social science doctoral student, he had no doubts about joining the graduate student union. Without hesitation, he became a member and an active participant in the group. He described himself as someone with a long personal history of engaging in social justice activism. He had also witnessed frequent strikes and student protest marches while he was an exchange student in Europe. He worked for a time as a writer for a progressive news media outlet and described himself as a liberal with progressive ideals of social justice.

Shortly after his arrival on campus, Tyler found that many students from his graduate department were heavily involved in the activities of the graduate student union. He was easily able to connect with students in his department and in other departments because of the bridges built through the meetings of the group. Tyler credited the graduate student union with creating a sense of community among academic disciplines that would have otherwise had little interaction because of the decentralized nature of the campus.

Tyler described how the graduate student union had recently become active and galvanized by new leadership after the previous leaders had left the organization. The graduate student union became energized with a renewed purpose, and he set about working behind the scenes to increase membership among all graduate students. Moreover, the graduate student union had a new issue of importance on its agenda: The university administration had recently implemented a revised graduate student financial aid policy.

The dean of the graduate school informed graduate students of the new financial aid policy through a memo that was sent out during the summer. The new policy stipulated that in the subsequent fall semester graduate students would receive fellowships rather than teaching assistantships. On the face of it, the new policy seemed to be advantageous for graduate students, as their stipends would not be tied to instructional duties. However, Tyler explained that it was actually a union-busting act that did not acknowledge the reality of the pressures that graduate students felt to teach classes, either for their own career development or from pressure within their departments. Tyler felt it was unjust that the memo was sent in the middle of the summer when most students had left campus. Students would have no recourse for voicing their opinion on the policy before it would be implemented. This action by the administration, Tyler felt, was a direct affront to a fair process and deliberately disregarded the views of graduate students even though the new policy would have a direct impact on them. In a statement prepared by the graduate student union and disseminated on its website, the members described this lack of consultation with the academic community by the administration as being secretive, rushed, and nondemocratic.

NEW DIRECTIONS FOR HIGHER EDUCATION • DOI: 10.1002/he

Tyler, along with other members of the graduate student union, resolved to create a counterpoint to the new graduate student financial aid policy so that they could make students aware of the hidden problems and unforeseen consequences for graduate students. The student union activists collaborated on creating a flyer, which was widely distributed around campus, that outlined the primary objections of the graduate student union to the financial aid policy changes. Changing the public perception of the new policy became Tyler's primary focus for the time that he was an active member of the graduate student union, and changes to the policy likewise became a rallying cry for the group, which became active once again after the period of dormancy following the strike.

As Tyler described it, and as it was confirmed by a memo distributed by the university administration, the changes to the graduate student financial aid policy purported to make graduate student teaching assistantships an optional part of students' academic trajectory. According to the dean's memo, the new policy would make students' awards completely fellowship based, and any teaching would be optional and paid in addition to the fellowship. The graduate students who taught would then be considered adjuncts, and as such, would be part of the adjunct union. In a statement responding to the new policy, the student union activists collectively stated that they thought the changes would have a negative effect on their ability to organize in the future.

According to Tyler, graduate students do not really have a choice in the matter of whether or not they teach courses. As Tyler described it, the culture of graduate school has many hidden pressures and unstated rules to which students must adhere or face possible negative consequences. For example, if a professor requests that a student teach a recitation session for a class, the student cannot realistically decline, considering the inherent power differential between faculty and graduate students. Students need to maintain good relationships with their professors because they will be in need of letters of recommendation and assistance in progressing through their degree program. Therefore, as Tyler stated, creating a policy in which graduate student teaching is on a voluntary basis is simply a ploy to undermine the union's efforts at organizing. According to Tyler, the changes to the student financial aid policy were simply a distraction—a way for the administration to cut labor costs while disempowering the organizing efforts of the graduate student union.

Tyler made it his mission to create a campaign of awareness regarding the revised financial aid policy, and he redoubled his efforts to get graduate students to sign union membership cards. These efforts were rewarded when the graduate student union finally was able to gather enough signatures to present its case for reconsideration. The graduate student union held a public event outside the campus library to celebrate this victory, which was attended by local media. Tyler, however, was disheartened by the administrator's reaction to the event. Tyler noted that the administration released a statement saying that it was perplexed by the actions taken by the graduate student union. In Tyler's view, the use of the term "perplexed" was yet another attempt by the university administration to disempower the movement created by the graduate student union. He felt that the term was used in a condescending, infantilizing way, as if the university administrators regarded the actions of the union members as irrational and not well thought out. According to Tyler, the administration tried to "make the graduate student union look kind of childish, like we hadn't really quite thought through these things, you know, sort of rowdy, not totally rational." Moreover, he believed the administration tried to express this to the university community.

However, Tyler reflected that this was the reaction that activists should come to expect from the university administration. More important, the graduate student union had gained the respect of a majority of the faculty and graduate students on campus in spite of the many challenges the union faced in its ongoing battle. This respect, Tyler felt, was not shared by the university administration but was something that kept him going even through the difficult times of the graduate student union's campaign.

Teaching and Learning Amid Conflict.   Rodney, another member of the graduate student union, described himself as someone who grew up with a propensity toward liberal, progressive political ideals, terms that he used to describe himself. When he arrived on campus to begin his doctoral program in the humanities, he felt it was a natural step for him to join the graduate student union and begin supporting the union's activities. However, he also described himself as someone with a more laissez-faire attitude toward the graduate student union movement and its goals. His role in the organization was one of support and advocacy behind the scenes. In other words, he was not a key player in the leadership or decision-making processes of the organization, although he attended most events to show his support and discuss union issues informally with his fellow graduate students.

As a doctoral student in the humanities, Rodney taught a number of undergraduate classes. Although Rodney described himself in terms of his liberal, progressive political stance, he took great pains to differentiate his personal viewpoints from his teaching. He did not want to appear to be advocating a liberal or progressive agenda. Rather, his goal as an instructor was to present relevant information to his students and encourage them to analyze the information with a critical eye. Whether or not he agreed with the students, he felt he had done his job if he could encourage them to think critically and analytically.

As an activist, albeit one who was more behind the scenes, Rodney felt that he had a duty to inform the undergraduate students of the circumstances that had brought about the actions of the graduate student union. For example, he felt it was important to raise awareness among the undergraduate students of the relatively large proportion of teaching performed by graduate teaching assistants and adjunct instructors. Rodney explained that undergraduates needed to understand where their tuition money was going and why the graduate student union members took the actions that they did. Rodney described a silent protest in which he was a participant: "We would go to the library and we'd sit on the benches at the main entrance and just grade silently and wear a [graduate student union] sign on our T-shirts. So all the students can see us, and they can read the signs. And that's a pretty important place on campus."

Although Rodney did not begin attending graduate school until a few years after the strike, he described how the organization's current actions made him reflect upon that incident. He did not think that the strike resulted in any significant advances for reaching the goals of the graduate student union, and so he was pleased with the recent progress that the organization had made, particularly in gaining enough union members to resubmit its case to the administration. Going through the proper legal channels in a systematic manner was the correct way to proceed with the graduate student union's mission, according to Rodney.

Conclusion

As higher education institutions become affected by financial crises and funding cuts, they are increasingly reliant on contingent faculty as well as graduate student labor to fulfill their educational mission (Bousquet & Nelson, 2008). Moreover, students are faced with increasing student debt and rising tuition costs. Yet, even within this reality, as the case studies herein have illustrated, graduate student union activists have struggled to transform their institutional working and learning environments against great odds.

In this study, graduate students voiced the opinion that there were too many impediments to achieving activist goals and missions through campus political activities. Therefore, student activists sought out ways in which they could participate in an alternative form of politics through off-campus organizations within the local community or through their own teaching. The students viewed activism as a training ground where they could learn skills that would assist them in tackling problems in their later careers. Extending what Hollander and Longo (2008) called a cynical regard for traditional politics but a high regard for community-based volunteer and political work, graduate students in this study reflected their understanding that they would eventually have to leave the campus environment in order to contribute to social change. Research by Ropers-Huilman, Barnett, and Carwile (2005) showed that student activists viewed their interactions with administrators on a spectrum that ranged from being collegial and supportive to being an unsympathetic, bureaucratic impediment to their activist mission. The students in the case studies similarly reported their interactions with administrators as being distant and bureaucratic in nature.

As in the past, student activists continue to bring important questions to the table and shine a light on the problems facing higher education today: Governance, finance, diversity, environmental issues, and the corporatization of higher education, among others, are all issues of great concern to the field of higher education policy and research (Dobbie & Robinson, 2008). Moreover, the presence of student activism is more than just an exercise in learning for the students who participate. Student activists put their own spin on the campus culture and environment, creating a sense of openness and interest in social problems that could be beneficial to all students. As Astin and Astin (2000) argued, it is essential for the development of leadership skills that students participate as leaders for change within their campus environment. The fact that this participation generates conflicts with the administration should not lessen its value. Regardless of the outcomes of graduate student union activism, such activities shed light on the problematic structure of higher education that has consequences for all stakeholders.

Implications for Practice.   When students feel compelled to join activist movements on campus, many learning opportunities arise, both for students and administrators. The students in these cases felt strongly that they contributed hard work in researching and organizing their campaign in order to present their case to the administration and the student body. While administrators face many constraints in their policymaking, they should hear and acknowledge the students' questions and concerns and include them in a democratic and collegial decision-making process. Furthermore, the administration could recognize the students' efforts as being a positive part of their overall learning experience and find ways to contribute positively to student activist efforts in a mutually beneficial way. Similarly, faculty, if supported by the administration, could play a much stronger role of mentorship for student activists. Thus, by uniting student activists, university administrators, and faculty behind common goals of advocacy for the improvement of the higher education learning environment, the synergistic benefit of activism could be realized.

References

Astin, A. W., & Astin, H. S. (2000). *Leadership reconsidered: Engaging higher education in social change*. Battle Creek, MI: Kellogg Foundation.

Bousquet, M., & Nelson, C. (2008). *How the university works: Higher education and the low-wage nation*. New York: New York University Press.

Dixon, M., Tope, D., & Dyke, N. V. (2008). "The university works because we do": On the determinants of campus labor organizing in the 1990s. *Sociological Perspectives, 51*(2), 375–396. doi:10.1525/sop.2008.51.2.375

Dobbie, D., & Robinson, I. (2008). Reorganizing higher education in the United States and Canada: The erosion of tenure and the unionization of contingent faculty. *Labor Studies Journal, 33*(2), 117–140.

Flora, B. H. (2007). Graduate assistants: Students or staff, policy or practice? The current legal employment status of graduate assistants. *Journal of Higher Education Policy and Management, 29*(3), 315–322.

Hollander, E., & Longo, N. V. (2008). Student political engagement and the renewal of democracy. *Journal of College and Character, 10*(1), 1–9.

National Labor Relations Board. (n.d.). *National Labor Relations Act.* Retrieved from http://www.nlrb.gov/resources/national-labor-relations-act

Rhoades, G., & Rhoads, R. A. (2002). The public discourse of U.S. graduate employee unions. *The Review of Higher Education, 26*(2), 163–186. doi:10.1353/rhe.2002.0035

Riessman, C. K. (2008). *Narrative methods for the human sciences.* Thousand Oaks, CA: Sage.

Ropers-Huilman, B., Barnett, K., & Carwile, L. (2005). Student activists' characterizations of administrators in higher education: Perceptions of power in "the system." *The Review of Higher Education, 28*(3), 295–312. doi:10.1353/rhe.2005.0012

Singh, P., Zinni, D. M., & MacLennan, A. F. (2006). Graduate student unions in the United States. *Journal of Labor Research, 27*(1), 55–73. doi:10.1007/s12122-006-1009-9

Wickens, C. M. (2008). The organizational impact of university labor unions. *Higher Education, 56*(5), 545–564.

HEIDI WHITFORD is an assistant professor in the higher education administration graduate program at Barry University in Miami Shores, Florida.

3

This chapter explores the ways faculty and staff work with students to support their activism as well as the way students tap faculty and staff to support their movements.

Collective Action on Campus Toward Student Development and Democratic Engagement

Adrianna Kezar, Dan Maxey

Campus activism has been part of college life for centuries (Astin, 1975; Hamrick, 1998). However, only recently have scholars and practitioners examined the ways activism can lead to student learning and development. The activism of the 1960s demonstrated the potential of activism to foster a sense of democratic participation and to help students explore ways to shape local, regional, and national politics, as well as social norms (Astin, 1975; Gaston-Gayles, Wolf-Wendel, Tuttle, Twombley, & Ward, 2004).

In this chapter, we build on this emerging understanding of the role of student activism in student development by examining the ways students can partner with faculty and staff on campus as a part of this learning process. Through reviewing the results of a study on grassroots leadership on college campuses, we describe the specific ways that partnering with faculty and staff creates deeper and broader learning outcomes for students. We also highlight how faculty and staff approach these partnerships as educators rather than pure activists, often working behind the scenes. Further, we suggest ways campuses can create an environment that fosters these types of partnerships that help students learn about democratic involvement. We believe that an environment that supports activism is one that has greater integrity and reflects the democratic ideals embraced by the United States. What better way for campuses to prepare students than to demonstrate and foster activism—one of the most important aspects of democratic engagement (McTighe-Musil, 2013)? Before presenting our research, we review some of the earlier studies that demonstrated the potential of activism to create learning as well as the few studies on collective action among faculty, staff, and students to improve student outcomes.

New Directions for Higher Education, no. 167, Fall 2014 © 2014 Wiley Periodicals, Inc.
Published online in Wiley Online Library (wileyonlinelibrary.com) • DOI: 10.1002/he.20103

Research on How Collective Action Among Faculty, Staff, and Students in Grassroots Leadership Supports Student Learning

Research demonstrates that activism is a vehicle for student learning about democratic process, citizenship, and leadership, an area of learning noted as being in decline nationally among students (Astin, 1975; Hamrick, 1998; Rhoads, 1998; Tsui, 2000). Interestingly, most of the research focuses on student activism in isolation of other stakeholder activism on campus. Neither the ways students partner with faculty and staff on campus to create change nor the roles of faculty and staff as mentors and partners for students' development through activism have been a part of these earlier studies.

Only a small number of studies have examined and shown the potential of faculty and staff for helping to create civic learning and democratic engagement through activism. Astin's (1975) case-study research suggests that students learn to vary their strategies by working with faculty; they become better able to make decisions about whether to persuade or take more coercive forms of demonstration to achieve their ends. Gaston-Gayles et al. (2004) noted that student affairs professionals periodically took an educational role to help students refine their requests to the administration, identify appropriate decision makers to consult, and help determine and craft appropriate solutions to their concerns. By being a resource for students on questions about leadership and organizational change, student affairs professionals help expose students to new opportunities to learn and develop. Rhoads, Saenz, and Carducci (2005) illustrated how students learn the importance of working in coalitions through collaboration with faculty and administrators in responding to the affirmative action case at the University of Michigan. In their research, they describe how administrators, faculty, and students worked together in a coalition, which they likened to a social movement, that was able to create greater change than if these groups had worked separately. They linked agendas, sought to overcome resistance through having greater numbers of individuals aligned, and aligned messages, for example.

Building on this limited set of studies, this chapter highlights our study that sought to examine ways that collective action leads to deep and broad learning among students and to pinpoint the variety and types of learning and ways faculty, staff, and students effectively work together. While earlier studies allude to the role of faculty or staff, none of them intended to try to understand the way such partnering supports student development; therefore, they garnered few details.

Collective Action to Learn Civic Engagement Strategies

Building on earlier research about how students learn from activism, we examined the benefits of collective action among faculty, staff, and students.

In this section, we describe research conducted on five campuses[1] examining some ways that faculty, staff, and students worked together to create change on their campus, in their communities, and across the nation; more than just supporting students' activism efforts, these collaborations and activities resulted in student development. We also describe the approaches the faculty and staff used as they created collective action with students and demonstrate the type of learning that occurred as a result of these strategies. The key learning outcomes that emerged in our study were (a) developing plans for change, (b) determining strategies, (c) learning approaches to consciousness raising, (d) learning the language of those in power and how "the system" works, (e) understanding mediation and negotiation, (f) using data to influence decision makers, and (g) navigating and overcoming obstacles in the change process. While the list of key learnings was long, we highlight some areas that help students learn to navigate as citizens and activists in the future.

Developing Plans for Change.   Students often approach change with a narrow set of strategies; sometimes they only have one approach in mind. Faculty and staff can help students to expand the repertoire of approaches they take for change and can help them to think about change as an ongoing process requiring retooling and shifting over time. On one campus where faculty and staff created a multicultural curriculum, it started with a small effort—working in ethnic studies developing support and advocacy. Eventually the faculty realized if they wanted the new curriculum to be integrated across the campus, they needed to engage the academic senate to implement broader curricular changes, alter hiring criteria, and develop mentoring programs. They created a plan to influence and lobby various faculty in schools and colleges and even wait for some retirements among faculty who resisted their efforts. There were state policies, such as Proposition 209, a state ban on the use of race/ethnicity in publically funded college admissions and scholarships, that appeared might support or hinder faculty and staff efforts at certain points in time. And, faculty/staff proponents had to get involved with state-level politics as well because state politics influence administrators and their willingness to provide resources and support for initiatives. Sharing examples of how plans develop and change over time and how new obstacles and power blocks can emerge also helps students to understand that activism and civic engagement are multifaceted, involve complex strategies, and shift as the efforts broaden.

Determining Strategies.   The study found that faculty and staff could also help students in identifying appropriate strategies that helped move students' efforts forward. On one of the campuses in the study, a group of students wanted to create a lesbian, gay, bisexual, and transgender (LGBT) center to better support students in the LGBT community. The students had offered several proposals to the administration without success; therefore, their focus was shifting toward protesting the administration. Staff members who were working with the students knew that resources were extremely limited at the institution and that office space or resources would be very difficult for almost any group to secure. They also knew from experience that campus administrators were not typically swayed by open protests and might instead dig in their heels in response. So, they suggested that the students should consider alternative strategies that might meet their objectives, which could involve creating and presenting a different proposal to the administration. The students' staff partners contacted the head of a research center on campus that focused on LGBT issues to solicit the center's input. Faculty members and staff decided that providing modest funding for student groups and connecting them to a campus-wide task force on LGBT issues could accomplish what the proposed center would do without the high cost. This proposal went to the administration and was approved. Through this process, students learned to examine multiple strategies and determine ones that would be most successful within their context.

Learning Approaches to Consciousness Raising. Students also tended to think narrowly about how to raise campus and public consciousness about their efforts or the issues they advocated; they mostly gravitated to direct action such as protests or contacting the media. Faculty and staff partners can help students understand that raising consciousness is important at multiple levels and often involves utilizing various strategies other than protests and contacting the media. Faculty and staff in the study talked about how they used individual strategies (e.g., one-to-one meetings, mentoring) to raise consciousness among colleagues. Sharing these experiences with students can help faculty and staff to see parallels to their own efforts. Faculty and staff also introduced other groups (such as alumni and community groups) and organizationally oriented activities (such as starting a speaker series or invited lunches) to help raise consciousness.

Holding protests and picketing can be important strategies to help make stakeholders aware of an issue, but the vitality and potential of these strategies for creating change can be diminished when they are the only ones used. For example, one campus in our study was trying to get more attention for the importance of immigration reform; individual students who were behind these efforts were disappointed that their fellow students were not as supportive as they had expected. While they garnered some media attention, they failed to foster a better understanding of the issues among their peers, which might have increased support for their efforts. Rather than allowing these students to give up, faculty and staff helped them find new ways to generate awareness by assisting them with sponsoring events, holding discussions in residence halls, and suggesting course assignments that could be incorporated in classes in order to get students supporting immigration reform to think about some of the more individual strategies to raise consciousness among their peers.

**Learning the Language of Those in Power and How "The System"
Works.** Another part of navigating the change process is learning the
language of those in power and the processes that make a system work.
Each campus has its own culture, systems, and processes that affect change
and are themselves changed in different ways. Power relations—who holds
power, who tries to obstruct change, who is apathetic, and so on—also vary
in these different contexts. Faculty and staff members gain knowledge of
these processes and how they are shaped by power relations on campus
over time. Faculty and staff map the political landscape on campus, either
formally or informally, and identify what the administration (and other faculty and staff) considers to be priorities, as compared to what it does not
value. By doing so, faculty and staff begin to understand how things work;
they become attuned to the type of language that tends to persuade those
in power. Although faculty and staff learn to navigate these conditions over
time, this whole landscape will be unfamiliar to many students. So, faculty
and staff are able to help students to be attentive to these conditions and
learn how to map the landscape and important processes or factors that
make the system work.

On one campus, a group of faculty, staff, and students was working
to create a community environmental initiative but found that their efforts
were being thwarted and community members began to pull away support.
Staff members began to look for some clues about people on campus who
might be poisoning the well. Through their campus network, they identified that a senior member of the administration and a vocal faculty member were planting seeds of doubt in the community. They were able to ob-
tain some information about their messaging (which was not public) so
they could counter their logic. For example, a senior faculty member might
be telling administrators that the students' recycling program is extremely
costly. Once student leaders recognize this false information is being shared,
they can correct administrators' impressions by letting them know the program's actual cost.

Understanding Mediation and Negotiation. Most students lack experience navigating complex institutional hierarchies; faculty and staff can
be instrumental in helping students understand how to approach the administration with their agenda and make progress through mediation, skills
that are beneficial to future work in their professions and in the community.
Sometimes, faculty and staff even help students negotiate with the administration. For example, on one campus, students (in conjunction with faculty
and staff) created a community farm, which was used to educate other students about organic farming. Campus administrators and local residents,
who were concerned that the farm was creating health and safety hazards,
wanted to shut it down. They were upset that homeless persons were stealing food from the farm and were beginning to loiter and leave waste around
the campus and the neighboring communities. The students did not mind
the homeless people using the farm and felt this added an additional benefit

NEW DIRECTIONS FOR HIGHER EDUCATION • DOI: 10.1002/he

of feeding the homeless, not an original goal, but it seemed a worthy one. Additionally, students did not see a problem with the homeless loitering on campus; they felt the administrators were being uptight and too worried about their image. The students did not want to negotiate with the administration, but their faculty and staff allies helped them to understand the administration's and community's concerns; they helped bring the students and administration together in order to make some compromises to allow the farm to remain, while addressing some of the health and safety issues that had been raised. Students reported a new awareness of the value of listening to concerns; they experienced how negotiation allowed both sides to address their concerns constructively.

Using Data to Influence Decision Makers.   Data can be an important tool for persuading people in positions of authority to take action and can be helpful in negotiating change. Faculty and staff help students to appreciate the potential for data to influence leaders, as well as helping them learn how to collect, analyze, and present data. For example, one group of students wanted to significantly reduce their campus's carbon footprint. The administration had been clear that it was not interested in changing its policies, but the students were determined to bring about a change. A faculty member saw an opportunity to help the students by creating projects that would connect their experience to the curriculum. He created an assignment for an upcoming course that would allow students to study the environmental impact of the campus such as its electrical or water usage. He recruited several of the students to enroll in the course who had been interested in the effort to reduce the carbon footprint. For the course assignments, the students participated in activities such as collecting benchmark data from other institutions, reviewing sustainability standards that were developed by environmental organizations, and studying how resources were used on the campus. To showcase their work and help get their data in front of decision makers, their professor arranged for the students to make a presentation to the trustees and the administration about the findings of their projects. The students' hard work paid off; the compelling data they collected and presented to the administration and board persuaded them to make some of the changes the students recommended. The students also learned how change can be affected by creating and using data to influence decision making.

Navigating and Overcoming Obstacles in the Change Process. Most students lack experience navigating complex institutional hierarchies and power conditions, so they do not always know how to respond to obstacles that are a natural part of the change process. These challenges can cause students who are new to activism to become disenchanted, particularly when the obstacles involve persons in positions of authority shutting down their ideas. Faculty and staff often helped students understand that these obstacles are a natural part of change and gave some strategies for addressing their frustrations. On one campus, students wanted to develop

Figure 3.1. Continuum of Faculty and Staff Involvement

| *More overt and open* | *Openly, but mostly as advisors* | *Behind the scenes* |

a leadership program, but the administration responded that they would not provide any support for the effort. The student leaders of the project felt they had tried many strategies but did not make any progress, so they wanted to just give up. Faculty in ethnic studies, political science, and sociology who had mentored the students to develop the proposal and staff in student affairs involved in service learning and civic engagement hosted a retreat for the student activists. At the retreat, they shared their own stories about failed attempts and the obstacles they overcame, which sometimes seemed insurmountable at the time, to create changes on their campuses. For example, some spoke about the struggles over 10 years to get multiculturalism added to the curriculum. By hearing faculty and staff describe their own "war stories," the students began to feel more empowered; they saw past their short-term setbacks and understood that through time and effort, they could realize their own goals for change.

Approaches to Working With Students

In addition to identifying some of the different ways faculty and staff foster students' development by assisting them with their activism, we also learned about how faculty and staff preferred to work with students. A study by Gaston-Gayles et al. (2004) noted that we need to better understand how faculty and staff effectively negotiate the tenuous position of being activists working alongside students given their roles as employees of their institutions. In each of the examples described previously, how directly or indirectly faculty and staff participated in the students' activism varied along a continuum with three key points, shown in Figure 3.1. First, some worked overtly with students and operated in the open by joining in protests and direct action. These more overt forms of involvement included faculty and staff calling for a meeting with the administration, sponsoring a major campus protest or forums, cowriting an editorial for a campus newspaper or regional newspaper, and the like. Second, they worked as collaborators but were less overtly involved and open in their role and activism strategies. Some faculty or staff might be aware a faculty activist is a club adviser, but many others would not be cognizant. Also, they would not be involved in protests and other similar activities. Third, faculty and staff were more or less behind the scenes so that other campus stakeholders may not have known who was involved and who was serving informally and unofficially as mentors to and advocates for the protest. The involvement of faculty and staff largely went unnoticed by others; the activism was seen as being a student-initiated and student-led effort.

On the continuum, faculty and staff tended to work behind the scenes or in the middle of the continuum as advisers and collaborators, rather than more overtly and openly, particularly when politically charged issues were involved. When the issue at the heart of the students' activism posed risks for their involvement (e.g., advocating for a position that might affect alumni giving or trustee support), faculty and staff felt a measured approach made more sense. They noted a desire to emphasize their roles as educators and less as activists. Faculty and staff expressed a preference for working with students through institutional channels and in educationally oriented ways; a goal of their participation was to foster student development by helping students to interpret the landscape, expand their repertoire of strategies, and consider alternatives or supplements to more direct forms of activism. Faculty and staff partners were less likely to be disparaged if they worked with students on issues or in ways that they could argue were educationally relevant, related to student development, and in which faculty and staff could demonstrate they were teaching the students important skills. Many faculty and staff commented how participating in activism in overt ways opened them up more to criticism from the administration and their colleagues.

It is important to note that because faculty and staff prefer to be more behind the scenes, it may not appear they are actively involved with students on campuses. It is therefore critical to reinforce the many formal or informal roles they have as advisers to campus groups, creating opportunities to raise consciousness in the classroom, and providing mentorship.

Characteristics of Campuses That Foster Greater Collective Action

Our study also revealed campus characteristics and practices that support collective action and can lead to these more robust learning outcomes for students, including a supportive institutional mission, curricula and cocurricula that foster forms of activism, the existence or creation of networks of activists, and hiring activists and socializing new employees to understand the importance of activism to student learning. While a campus environment does not need to have all of these characteristics, most of them are present on campuses where collective action is more the norm. Efforts to help incorporate these features on other campuses can help to improve the ability for faculty and staff to partner with students as a way to support their learning and development.

Mission.   First, on these campuses student activism and leadership are seen as a primary objective; they are part of the mission and goals. Campus leaders in the study noted the connection of activism with political engagement and made conscious efforts to support the development of these skills. Leaders would speak about activism as a natural part of campus

learning and encourage participation as a way to enact democratic involvement at events such as convocation, orientation, and graduation. Campus
leaders also invite activists to campus to give speeches at major events.
Leaders also encouraged faculty and staff to play the role of mentors, guides,
and advisers for students.

Formal and Informal Curriculum. When an institution's mission
and goals are oriented toward fostering activism as a form of civic engagement, informal and formal curricula emphasizing grassroots leadership and
activism are developed in a more organic way to support those objectives,
too. Many faculty in the study talked about how their formal curriculum
included learning the skills to be activists such as strategies, consciousness-
raising activities, or how to navigate power relations. Others, who were
advisers to student clubs, noted how they saw themselves as informally
teaching students about activist skills, no matter what the content or focus
of the student club happened to be. Faculty and staff also described how
they met informally over lunches and discussion groups to talk about approaches and strategies they would use with students to help them learn to
be an activist or engaged citizen in society. They shared tips around developing a successful curriculum and cocurriculum aimed at fostering collective
action.

Networks. Another feature that supports collective action is when
individuals on campus create networks to connect faculty, staff, and students with similar interests—be it sustainability, immigration reform, multiculturalism, political engagement, interdisciplinarity, wellness, or work-
life balance. Campuses where activism is a part of the ethos create channels
for communication so that people with similar interests can connect with
each other. They also try to develop informal pathways for meeting (e.g.,
lunch groups, book groups) where people can meet on their shared topic
of interest from time to time and think about ways to address a concern
like sustainability; this may grow to involve various forms of activism over
time.

Hiring and Socialization. Such campuses also tend to hire individuals who have a history or experience as a student or community activist.
Hiring committees looked for people who had made changes in other communities or organizations that they had been a part of and saw this as a
desirable feature for their new colleagues. Furthermore, once people were
hired they could be mentored by others who have an appreciation of how
the campus and local community operates, helping them to navigate these
environments to be an effective activist. One way to socialize new members
of the campus community that was noted in the study was through holding events that involve discussion of issues that people are passionate about.
On these campuses, groups routinely sponsored talks and speakers that fea-
tured themes of political participation and activism; they were constantly
engaged in discussion about the important issues of the time, whether it

was human rights, immigration, sustainability, poverty, or matters of public health.

Conclusion

In this chapter, we have focused on demonstrating the benefits of collective action among campus activists for student learning. Reviewing the various types of learning outcomes helps faculty and staff identify some of the roles they might play and ways to focus their efforts. We also demonstrated faculty and staff members' desire to play a more behind-the-scenes role or be a collaborator/mentor/adviser, positions that were seen as less politically dangerous and perhaps as more educationally defensible. In this behind-the-scenes role, they found themselves less open to critique from internal and external campus stakeholders. In the last section, we highlighted ways administrators and leaders might support this learning through the campus mission and goals, curricular and cocurricular realignment, creation of campus networks, and hiring and socialization processes. Collective action among faculty, staff, and students furthers student development and learning. Furthermore, collective action also helps campuses meet their mission of political engagement and democratic involvement and participation. We hope to encourage all stakeholders on campus to foster collective activism for the many benefits it affords students.

Note

1. In order to understand more about faculty and staff grassroots leadership/activism (we use these two terms interchangeably), we conducted case studies of five typical institutions of higher education representing different sectors (community college, liberal arts college, private research university, technical university, and regional public university—two were unionized, three were not) assuming that grassroots leadership might differ by institutional type. We are interested in examining and understanding the bottom-up leadership efforts of faculty and staff working within "typical" institutions of higher education (i.e., those institutions not characterized by an institutional commitment to innovation, activism, and change). We interviewed 165 grassroots leaders—84 staff and 81 faculty members—at five different institutions (typically 33 individuals per institution) engaged in grassroots leadership.

References

Astin, A. (1975). *Power of protest*. San Francisco, CA: Jossey-Bass.

Gaston-Gayles, J., Wolf-Wendel, L., Tuttle, K., Twombley, S., & Ward, K. (2004). From disciplinarian to change agent: How the civil rights era changed the roles of student affairs professionals. *NASPA Journal, 42*(3), 263–282.

Hamrick, F. (1998). Democratic citizenship and student activism. *Journal of College Student Development, 39*, 449–460.

McTighe-Musil, C. (2013). *A crucible moment*. Washington, DC: Association of American Colleges and Universities.

Rhoads, R. (1998). *Freedom's web: Student activism in an age of cultural diversity.* Baltimore, MD: Johns Hopkins University Press.

Rhoads, R., Saenz, V., & Carducci, R. (2005). Higher education reform as a movement: The case of affirmative action. *The Review of Higher Education, 28*(2), 191–220.

Tsui, L. (2000). Effects of campus culture on student's critical thinking. *The Review of Higher Education, 23*(4), 421–441.

ADRIANNA KEZAR is a professor of higher education at the University of Southern California.

DAN MAXEY is a doctoral candidate at the University of Southern California.

This chapter elaborates on the range of collective action tactics and organizing strategies that today's students invoke to pursue their ambitions for social change.

Campus-Based Organizing: Tactical Repertoires of Contemporary Student Movements

Cassie L. Barnhardt

Introduction

More than 50 years ago, university leaders and the general public expressed concerns that the campus activism of the free speech, civil rights, and Vietnam eras posed a threat to campus and public safety (American Council on Education, 1970). Amid these concerns, the U.S. Senate Committee on Government Operations conducted a study accounting for all the campus riots and disorders that occurred between the fall of 1967 and spring of 1969 (Harris, 1969). This process documented 471 incidences occurring on 211 U.S. campuses with students engaging in public demonstrations, occupying spaces (buildings, offices, streets), boycotting classes, disrupting college extracurricular activities, and holding hostages. About one third of these campus incidences involved damage of some kind including bombings or attempted bombings, arson or suspected arson, property damage, or personal injury. In total, 6,158 arrests were reported as a consequence of the wave of campus protests from 1967 to 1969. The lingering residue of this tumultuous time period in U.S. history has been described as imparting society with "a set of terms and impressions" about campus activism that have since been ingrained in our culture (Zald, 1996).

Today, the sociopolitical issues that fuel particular campus organizing efforts have changed from the topics pursued 40 years ago, but the substantive task of needing to understand how college students pursue their collective ambitions for change remains a salient matter for campus educators and administrators, as well as for the students themselves. Views about campus mobilizing have evolved from being seen as problematic and something administrators must *deal* with (Scranton, 1970), to being concomitant with students' learning about and subsequently acting on democratic and

NEW DIRECTIONS FOR HIGHER EDUCATION, no. 167, Fall 2014 © 2014 Wiley Periodicals, Inc.
Published online in Wiley Online Library (wileyonlinelibrary.com) • DOI: 10.1002/he.20104

civic ideals (Hamrick, 1998; Hunter, 1988). This chapter draws attention to the enactment of college students' social change ambitions by examining what the study of collective action tells us about tactics, and how students employ tactics in contemporary campus contexts. Admittedly, college students' participation in social movement action (both historically and contemporarily) can exceed the geographic perimeters of the campus confines. For the purposes of procedural clarity then, the tactics discussed in this chapter are limited to those actions occurring within the physical or virtual boundaries of the campus.

Contemporary College Student Activism and Tactical Displays

Altbach and Cohen (1990) argue that the contentious and violent tactics of the late 1960s (described previously) were counterproductive for sustaining a robust ethos for student activism on campus as the 1970s brought on a marked decline in campus organizing. Even so, since the 1970s, numerous examples point to a steady flow of college student activism. In the 1980s, students pushed universities to divest their endowments from South Africa as an act of solidarity in support of the antiapartheid resistance movement; the 1990s were peppered with students organizing around the Persian Gulf war, working to expand the college curriculum (particularly in cultural and ethnic studies), protesting tuition increases, and marching to express concerns related to students' identities and the quality of the campus climate for underrepresented groups (Astin, Astin, Bayer, & Bisconti, 1997; Boren, 2001; Rhoads, 1998; Soule, 1997). More recently, student activists have expressed concerns about issues such as rising tuition and student debt (Brennan, 2012), campus fossil fuel investments (Gardner, 2013), access and opportunity for immigrant students (Jesse, 2012), and sexual assault on campus (Ramer, 2013).

Defining and Describing Tactics.   In the study of social movement phenomenon, collective action is evaluated according to its component parts. The elements include deconstructing collective action according to who specifically is seeking a change (*mobilizing group or groups*), the entity whom the mobilizing group aspires to influence (*targets*), the *claims* (or substantive ideas being advanced), and the *tactics* used in advancing the group's claims. Tactics are the particular actions and behaviors used to communicate the group's message. Together these four pieces coalesce to form an overall strategy that is enacted to work toward bringing about a desired change in the "social structure or reward distribution, or both" (McCarthy & Zald, 1987, p. 20). Tilly (2004) is careful to note that movements are distinct from other forms of similar political behavior (e.g., trade union activities or electoral campaigns) by virtue of the interaction of these aforementioned elements. At times tactics have also been described as *repertoires of contention*, a phrase used to denote the range of forms and combinations of behaviors that a movement group engages in (or might use if so desired; Tilly, 2004). Tactics operate as a public expression—by a group—that challenges the taken-for-granted authority relationships (Hirsch, 1999) and results in generating varying degrees of uncertainty, challenge, and solidarity within a particular social context (Tarrow, 1998). Tactics derive their meaning relative to the specific structural and cultural features of the environment or context that the movement group seeks to influence and can be generally categorized as being either violent, disruptive, conventional, or a combination of these things (Tarrow, 1998). Mueller's (1992) synthesis suggests that violent tactics occur when prior tactical approaches have failed in an overall protest cycle; that is, earlier approaches have not garnered sufficient public attention, provoked change, or elicited the engagement of those in power. In fact, in the civil rights era the nonviolent philosophy, which served to frame the tactical approaches in the early 1960s, precipitated the subsequent violence that manifested in the 1967 to 1969 protest cycle on campuses (Benford & Snow, 1992; McAdam, 1983).

It is not requisite for a tactic to be violent to make an impact on a target. However, tactics tend to be more resonant when they cultivate disruption. Disruption is achieved when a particular mobilizing group's action (e.g., rally, sit-in, boycott, teach-in, political theatre) prompts a reaction from a target, be it the state, the campus administration, or a group of likely sympathizers (student peers) with the movement's cause. Therefore, disruption occurs when a tactic simply "breaks the routine, startles bystanders, and leaves elites disoriented, at least for a time" (Tarrow, 1998, p. 104). Disruptive tactics get people talking, thinking, or responding to the mobilizing group's substantive claims. Conventional tactics are behaviors that elaborate or rely on existing routines and come with a preestablished set of norms or meanings. Conventional tactics are often endorsed or facilitated by the group that is being targeted such as when a mobilizing group chooses to express an alternative point of view at an annual event, standing meeting, or through regular organizational activities. Therefore, a strike/work stoppage may be a conventional tactic when the mobilization is directed toward a corporate employer, whereas the distribution of information leaflets may be a conventional tactic when the mobilization is directed toward a neighborhood association. On campus, conventional tactics could consist of numerous acts including student activists speaking during the university's governing board's open-comment time while like-minded activists sport T-shirts or signs with pithy slogans exemplifying the substantive claims being asserted. Through events such as these, campus activists capitalize on established forums, or conventional venues, to pursue their movement's ambitions.

The ability of mobilizing groups to use conventional approaches to achieve maximum disruption with a specific social context is perhaps one of the most critical aspects of movement strategy. Insider groups often have an advantage, compared to external/outsider mobilizing groups, because of the greater familiarity, legitimacy, and cultural knowledge of the organization they are targeting. Insider groups are those parties who are already established actors within an organization (in the case of campuses these would include stakeholder entities, such as students, faculty, alumni, staff, board members, etc.). Higher education institutions are thus more likely to experience challenges from insiders than from outsiders, and correspondingly, colleges are more likely to be subjected to the conventional tactics that build on the identities, behaviors, and values that the organization affirms and cultivates (Walker, Martin, & McCarthy, 2008). Walker and colleagues are careful to highlight, however, that insiders are quite capable of incorporating confrontation into conventional tactical approaches, which is why they prefer to describe tactics as existing along a continuum from being contained to being transgressive. Contained tactics tend to adapt to existing political process models or institutionalized modes of resolving conflict, whereas transgressive tactics tend to innovative or burst onto the scene in sporadic ways marking paradigmatic changes that bring about new frames of meaning or new actors to the substantive issue or overall protest cycle and dynamics (Tarrow, 1998; Walker et al., 2008).

In essence, contemporary college students, as organizational insiders, have privileged access to preexisting meanings of organizational routines and behaviors. They can then use this knowledge as a form of cultural competence for selecting their repertoires of contention (Clemens, 2004) for maximum impact upon their targets, who are often campus administrators. Arguably, the insider status that students currently possess may, in fact, be the byproduct of the campus violence associated with the late 1960s activism. Numerous scholars have highlighted the discernible shift from the punctuated violent tactics of the 1960s toward a softened or tamer approach in student activists' tactics since that time (Altbach & Cohen, 1990; Astin et al., 1997). It is feasible that the magnitude of the transgressive disruption from the 1960s violence reframed meaning in a transformative way—repositioning students' status from that of being outside the channels of campus organizational power to a new order that situated students as legitimate stakeholders with tangible power on campus. Social movement scholars have argued that a generalized softening of tactics has occurred in U.S. society in the post-1960s timeframe as the United States has expanded its basis of political organizing structures, moving from spontaneous outsider groups using tactics to express their grievances against the state, to a range of member-based interest groups engaged in sustained advocacy as a recurring component of democratic and civic life (Meyer & Tarrow, 1998; Soule & Earl, 2005). Zald and Berger (1978) characterize this transformation in social structure as a bureaucratization of discontent to describe how insiders use existing structures and organizational knowledge to engage in tactics for the purpose of bringing about changes in some aspect of organizational functioning. For student activism, it is possible to envision a similar phenomenon with the formal expansion of student identity-based and interest-based groups that have proliferated and diversified on campus in the past several decades as changes in enrollment patterns have brought greater racial, ethnic, geographic, and class-based diversity to campus, and as extracurricular opportunities have grown (Altbach, 2006).

Factors That Shape Campus Tactics. Theory tells us that student movements will be efficacious in advancing their claims when they are skillful in properly matching their tactics to the substantive issue and to the intended audience. Klandermans (2004) asserts that the viability of a movement tactic is predicated on criteria such as organizational history and culture. For campuses, distinctive tradition, culture, curriculum, characteristics, and behavioral norms are some of the most foundational elements of higher education institutions (Clark, 1972; Kuh, Schuh, Whitt, & Associates, 1991). Mobilizing groups (student activists) are embedded in their campus communities where their interests are conditioned by the institutional context including its history, norms regarding moral indignation or injustice, individual and collective identities, and the social construction of emotions (Goodwin, Jasper, & Polletta, 2004; Klandermans, 2004; Kurzman, 2008). Campus activists can gain legitimacy with their targets (administrators and peers) when they anchor their tactical approaches to the master frames that are promoted in familiar rhetoric, policy, or administrative practice (Benford & Snow, 1992). Einwohner and Spencer's (2005) work highlighted the ways in these dominant master frames in use on campus shaped students' tactical displays. In their qualitative study of two structurally similar campuses, the campus culture that espoused a values-based problem-solving approach was associated with activists pursuing conventional tactics such as awareness campaigns and negotiating with administrators to seek procedural changes. When the local campus culture emphasized an overriding rational basis for decision making, activists pursued more disruptive forms of dissent including a sit-in, hunger strike, and demonstrations. This work emphasizes the ways in which tactics build on existing ideologies and correspond to broader cultural themes and values (Klandermans, 2004). This does not suggest that the viability of a given tactic presumes compatibility or conformity to the existing norms of conduct on campus. Rather, campus activists can finesse their tactical displays by choosing conventional activities of campus life and imbuing them with new meanings so they disrupt administrators' and peers' understandings of social life or organizational practices. That is, the student activists' task is to transform the mundane into the profane so that it compels campus administrators and/or peers to respond, or to take ameliorative action.

Research on tactics highlights the extent to which the tactics exhibited in a single event can be reflective of a larger, more geographically dispersed movement network (Smith, 2001; Soule, 1997). This has been well documented in a study of the shantytown protests that took place across U.S. college and university campuses in the late 1980s (Soule, 1997). Distinctive campus features such as offering a liberal arts curriculum and being more selective were associated with similar tactical displays (Soule, 1997). Other work has suggested that tactical displays are class-based, with middle-class collective action tending to take on a beneficent or philanthropic tone and largely consisting of conventional forms such as telephone canvassing or awareness campaigns (Mueller, 1992; Oliver & Marwell, 1988). Both of these patterns reflect that the choice of tactics that student activists adopt is partially influenced by external factors. Federated interest-based or ideological organizations, as well as philanthropic foundations, have long provided organizational advice to campus movement groups. Both left- and right-leaning organizations advise similar tactics to the pursuit of very different causes (Cowan et al., 1995; Gora, Goldberger, Stern, & Halperin, 1991; Smith, 1993; Stefancic & Delgado, 1996). Binder and Wood's (2012) recent research provides an intimate look at the ways in which conservative organizations and their thought leaders have worked to prepare college students for ideologically based activism on their campuses and in the wider community. This work points to many examples of conservative students being conflicted with the tactical advice coming from the parent organization that encourages confrontational and transgressive tactics, when students' preference is to engage in more conventional tactics that are more compatible with campus norms (Binder & Wood, 2012).

Campus Tactics in Comparative Contexts

I now turn to two examples of research that provide insights into how college student activists are advancing their social change ambitions through tactical displays on campus. The first example provides comparative insights based on a survey of campus administrators that reported on forms of tactics that college students have used over a 20-year period. The second example reflects the driving tactical approaches that students utilized in the college student antisweatshop campaign from 1998 to 2002.

Tactical Forms Utilized by Contemporary Student Activists.   In 2010, a random sample of U.S. four-year public and private college campuses was surveyed for the purpose of inquiring about various forms of tactical behaviors that college students utilized on their campuses to pursue their social change ambitions. For each campus, an informed respondent was identified to participate in the survey. In nearly all cases, this most knowledgeable person was the senior student affairs officer (vice presidents of student affairs and deans of students); in a few instances the senior student affairs officer redirected the survey to an alternate staff member who possessed the appropriate institutional memory to report on student activism patterns during the 20-year time period (1989–2010). Survey items presented respondents with an array of possible tactical approaches. Respondents were asked to identify which forms of activism or tactics students on their campuses had utilized over the years in question. Staff members were also asked to rate the tone of the activism and to provide information

NEW DIRECTIONS FOR HIGHER EDUCATION • DOI: 10.1002/he

Table 4.1. Percentage of Campuses Experiencing Specific Tactical Displays From Student Activists From 1989 to 2010

Tactic	Percentage
Petitioning	71.1
Rallies	56.6
Letter-writing campaign	51.3
Protests	34.2
Demonstrations	30.3
Leafleting	27.6
Pamphleteering	26.3
Political theatre	18.4
Press conferences	15.8
Teach-ins	15.8
Sleep-ins	13.2
Boycotts	10.5
Sit-ins	9.2
Pursuing law suits	6.6
Strikes	3.9
Building blockade/riot/attack/lie-in	1.3

Source: N = 79, four-year public and private campuses.

about the range of topics associated with contemporary campus-based mobilization activities. Overall, the survey yielded a 53% response rate from the sample group of campuses, for a total of 79 campuses responding. These 79 colleges and universities were representative of the randomly drawn sample according to campus characteristics such as institutional type, size, selectivity, geographic location, history of experiencing civil rights era protest, and the types of state-level statutory restrictions on campus dissent.

Survey findings revealed that from 1989 to 2010, petitioning was the most common tactic used on campuses to mobilize around a cause (see Table 4.1). The vast majority of all campuses experienced this approach, with 71% citing the occurrence of petitioning. Only two other tactics were displayed on a majority of campuses in the sample: 57% indicated that they experienced rallies, and 51% reported that students used letter-writing campaigns. These data further indicate that one third of all campuses experienced student protest or demonstration in the 20-year period, and one fourth reported that their students engaged in distributing leaflets and pamphlets in this same timeframe. When campus administrators were asked to evaluate the scope of the impact that students' tactics had on the campus, 44% of campus administrators reported that few or no members of the campus community noticed the mobilization.

Based on the reports of campus administrators, the use of violent tactics by activist college students was rare over the 20-year period. Riots and attacks were only reported at one campus in the sample. Likewise, 92% of administrators indicated that the tone of students' activism was best described as having been "orderly and peaceful." Only 5.3% of campuses reported that their students' activism resulted in creating an "uncomfortable" tone on campus, and none of the campuses chose the response options of "disruptive" or "violent or fearsome." These findings strongly support the idea that insiders utilize conventional tactics and campus activists tend to pursue contained rather than transgressive tactical approaches. Lawsuits were another tactical approach that student activists rarely deployed, with just slightly less than 7% of campuses reporting activism that unfolded in this manner. This finding is compatible with Walker et al.'s (2008) work noting that college students are less likely to pursue lawsuits, at least compared to their nonstudent counterparts such as outsider external organizations. Administrators indicated that strikes were a seldom-utilized tactic, with only 4% of campuses reporting having experienced a strike in the 20-year time period covered by the survey. The relative low occurrence of strikes is to be expected on account of strikes connoting work stoppages, and an accompanying labor relationship between parties. The nature of the student–university relationship (with the notable exception of graduate student labor; see Rhoads & Rhoades, 2005) does not satisfy the requisite political-opportunity structure required for matching the strike tactic to the institutional context.

Tactics Utilized Within a Specific College Student Movement. The campus tactics that college students used in the antisweatshop movement from 1998 to 2002 were evaluated as part of a larger mixed-method study examining contemporary campus mobilization (Barnhardt, 2012). The findings presented here were based on a dataset of 638 local, regional, and national newspaper articles that described all campus-based antisweatshop activities occurring across a sample of 149 four-year public and private colleges and universities. In total, 15% of the sample organized for the antisweatshop cause, resulting in news and opinion articles recounting instances of antisweatshop activity on 23 campuses. The articles were analyzed using protest event analysis or the process of compiling and classifying news accounts of mobilization activities that are dispersed over geographic time and space (Koopmans & Rucht, 2002). This method is a content-analytical technique to systematically organize the component properties of movement action and has been used as a staple of social movement research (Earl, Martin, McCarthy, & Soule, 2004; McCarthy, Martin, & McPhail, 2007; Tilly, 2004; Walker et al., 2008).

Context.   In the mid-1990s, major U.S. retailers (Disney, JC Penney, and Bloomingdales) and celebrity-endorsed clothing lines made news because of their entanglement with sweatshop-made apparel that was being manufactured both domestically and abroad (Apgar, 1995). In 1996, in response to mounting consumer outrage and with backing from the Clinton White House, the U.S. Department of Labor began working with garment manufacturers, labor leaders, and human rights groups to establish an organization that came to be known later as the Fair Labor Association (FLA;

Saucier, 1998). The group's purpose was to ensure that manufacturers complied with a code of conduct that addressed a range of issues from worker health and safety to child labor, freedom of association, collective bargaining, and antiharassment practices (Ross, 2003). No sooner was the FLA code established than faith and labor groups began to highlight its flaws, which included the lack of external monitoring to check that garment factories were adhering to the provisions outlined in the code (Esbenshade, 2004). In the summer of 1997, the antisweatshop cause gained momentum within the field of higher education. A small group of college student summer interns working for the Union of Needletrades, Industrial, and Textile Employees (UNITE) joined forces to explore whether their campus-branded athletic apparel had ties to the sweatshop manufacturing (Boris, 2002); they concluded that ties existed. By the fall of 1998, college students began organizing in response to the shortcomings of the FLA code, demanding that their collegiate-branded apparel be produced under sweat-free conditions. Students' efforts contributed largely to the creation of the Workers Rights Consortium (WRC), an entity conceived with the specific purpose to ensure that labor codes were enforced in university-branded apparel manufacturing (Featherstone & United Students Against Sweatshops, 2002; Ross, 2004). From 1998 to 2002, the college antisweatshop activists worked to urge campus administrators to sign on to the WRC, thus exerting the financial power and brand recognition of their universities in ways that could influence the garment industry more broadly to engage in humane labor practices. In 2002, the FLA changed its position on external monitoring, prompting a new phase of labor and human rights organizing on college campuses that wasn't so exclusively tied to the garment industry (Featherstone, 2003).

The college student antisweatshop movement was sandwiched between the student divestment movement from the 1980s that was principally concerned with the social responsibility of college endowment investments (i.e., divesting from any financial ties to apartheid South Africa; Soule, 1997) and a resurgence in graduate student labor union mobilization and campus labor organizing in general (Rhoads & Rhoades, 2005). The antisweatshop problem itself intersected with an array of students' interests, involving strands related to human rights, labor and trade policy, gender and women's equity, immigrant rights, environmental sustainability, and social justice. This intersection compelled students from a range of campus organizations to become involved as allies in the campus mobilization activities. Campus clubs included newly formed organizations with a loose organizational apparatus (e.g., Student Labor Action Coalition, No Sweat!), to preexisting clubs (Amnesty International), to mainstream long-established groups such as student government.

(Re)branding Meaning Through Symbols.   In the antisweatshop movement, student activists pursued tactics that were highly effective at pointing out inconsistencies between a college or university's espoused values and

those that were enacted through their apparel and licensing agreements. Many of the critiques consisted of forms of political theatre, creating displays that contrasted the integrity of the school's brand/logo and the labor abuses associated with the manufacturing of the apparel. Displays consisted of things such as creating clotheslines of university-branded apparel in common areas of campus and labeling the pieces with the wages that workers' received for making the items. On other campuses, students performed sweatshop fashion shows outside the main campus administration building or on the quad. Fashion shows consisted of modeling outfits, and then removing the university-branded pieces that were likely to have been made in a foreign sweatshop. Such tactics were an effective tool for the activists on account of their abilities to merge likeable trends in college-youth culture, such as fashion, popular dance music for the "catwalk," and school pride, with a stinging message about how campus apparel was being made. In another instance, activists used the campus homecoming parade to urge the administration to join the WRC and to cultivate public awareness of the sweatshop problem. In the parade, students created a caricature of a battle between students wearing only their boxers or underwear while chained to a shopping cart that was held by another student dressed as the Chairman of Nike. With this type of tactic, students put a twist on a typically lighthearted display of campus pride with floats of the homecoming team's mascot battling the opponent's mascot by offering a different type of battle. The "antisweatshop battle" tied the symbolic honor and integrity associated with the university logo to seemingly incongruent foes. A student activist, commenting on the choice to use tactics involving the logo, shared with the local newspaper: "Every student has some kind of [university] clothing, but we have little idea under what conditions these items are made.... The college shirts and hats that we wear with pride shouldn't be manufactured in demeaning and abusive conditions" (Collier, 1999, para. 4).

Political-theatre tactics remained a central component of the antisweatshop cause beyond just the focus on university institutional logos; other symbols of the textile industry offered innovative tactical messaging as well. Campus mobilization events included peaceful "knit-ins" along with variations on the sit-in and sleep-in tactic. Activists created symbolic scenes depicting the plight of sweatshop working conditions such as creating a mock sweatshop outside the dean's office and a makeshift hut outside the president's office to communicate the terrible conditions of textile workers. These sit-ins became sustained occupations of campus spaces in a few instances. Even in such contexts, the occupations remained peaceful and were generally nondisruptive to the normal proceedings of university life. Antisweatshop organizers also staged campus rallies, consisting of the routine components of such public displays, including brandishing signs, offering speeches, and chanting, but these displays were also peppered with theatrical elements. Rallies occurred in tandem with the aforementioned fashion shows where students stripped to their underwear to symbolize their indignation with the labor conditions thus choosing to "wear nothing" versus wearing items produced in sweatshops. On other campuses, rallies took on a livelier tone (much like that of a sports pep rally) and promoted awareness of labor abuses through gestures such as presenting a giant check to the university president for 3 cents or the amount of payment a worker would receive for a $15 to $20 T-shirt. Although not political theatre, antisweatshop organizers infused textile themes into routine tactics such as petition and letter-writing drives by crafting the slips of signatory paper in the shape of T-shirts in the school's colors so as to have maximum symbolic effect when these were delivered to campus administrators.

Normative Routines.   One of the most foundational tactical approaches campus antisweatshop activists employed was educating and informing the campus community about the antisweatshop cause. Tactics included producing extensive research reports on the substantive problem and submitting these to campus administrators; sending a few activist students on fact-finding trips abroad to collect data on the factories that were complicit in manufacturing university apparel under sweatshop conditions (some of which were pursued through formal study abroad experiences); and holding educational conferences locally or in cooperation with other nearby campuses to teach the campus community about the sweatshop problem. By and large, one tactic stood out as the most common approach to antisweatshop mobilization; this was hosting panels and/or sponsoring intellectual forums on campus for the purpose of cultivating a conversation about the sweatshop problem and the range of accompanying lenses through which the issues could be evaluated and analyzed. Still other antisweatshop tactics fit neatly into the regular routines and activities of campus life as organizers pursued the passage of student government resolutions calling for administrative action on the sweatshop issue, and penned letters to the editor explaining and commenting on their substantive concerns about sweatshops.

The ubiquity of students' choosing tactics that were highly compatible with the norms of campus life emphasizes the extent to which students worked from their insider status as members of the campus community to seek change. These educational tactics were both conventional and tended to be contained. Even so, the cultural symbols that antisweatshop activists used to amplify their cause took on a more transgressive quality. Homecoming parades and rallies were used in a conventional way by activists for they took advantage of the formal opportunities for student clubs and groups to display pride in their school or to gather together for a common cause on the campus quad. However, through conventional tactics, the student activists were successful in turning the normative meanings on their heads to dramatically reframe and disrupt the taken-for-granted views of campus pride. Activists offered a challenge to the way the community viewed its college T-shirts and university logos broadly, suggesting that they were morally suspect on account of the school being complicit in a supply chain that included questionable labor practices. Likewise, by challenging the existing meanings, they challenged campus leaders to take action to restore the dignity of their institutional brands.

Concluding Thoughts

Contemporary campuses have some influence over determining the parameters of collective action tactics. Campuses have adopted rules and regulations that outline appropriate conduct for students' freedom of expression and dissent; these guidelines typically are codified in university policies specifying the acceptable time, place, and manner of such actions (Bussian, 1995; Davis, 2004). Policies are designed to conform to the interests of the safety and well-being of the campus community and to affirm the ideal that the academic space is a robust arena for dissenting views (Bernstein, 2001). That said, dissent by its very nature is disobedient, and therefore, it is often communicated by taking actions or exhibiting behaviors that exceed the established boundaries of normative meanings. Innovative transgressive tactics that fall outside the confines of campus regulations for expression and dissent can be creative, culturally resonant, and perhaps more likely to engage others on the substantive movement issue. The tactics adopted in the student antisweatshop movement were especially representative of such an approach.

For some student activists, a set of campus speech guidelines is nothing more than a manual of conformist behaviors—something that is largely antithetical to campus activists' social change ambitions. On the other hand, campus policies regarding acceptable conduct for tactical expression provide a template for action specifying how to address controversy and how to dissent respectfully. Campus policies are designed to be proactive and rational, and they make assumptions about what tactics dissenters will use—namely, formal protests or gathering in or on campus common spaces. If future student activists continue to adopt the tactical approaches described in the theory and research presented in this chapter, administrators (and the policies they design) may be less adept at anticipating when, where, and how disruptions will occur. If everyday, conventional routines of college or university life are the contemporary venues for largely peaceful tactical maneuvers, then the rational processes documented in campus policies, such as advanced registration to gather in a public space or specifying the types of signs that can be brandished (sticks or no sticks, for example), may not be as useful as they were at another point in history. These days it seems the homecoming parade, student organization office space sign-up, an open governing board meeting, or the prospective student weekend forum have all become tactical opportunities to use conventional opportunities to impart alternative views and assert movement claims.

The research presented here tells us that campus tactics tend to be conventional, but they don't have to be contained. College student activists' tactics are largely peaceful, but the peacefulness should not be construed as inconsequential. Contemporary campus tactics may be disruptive and transgressive, but it takes a great deal of creativity and skillful timing to produce such meanings from everyday occurrences. That said, there are student activists that continue to engage in traditionally disruptive tactics or those behaviors that take on the form of civil disobedience. Sit-ins and occupations in various forms are very much alive and well in activist circles and remain to be part of the tactical repertoire of contemporary college students.

Finally, it is worthy of mention that issueless riots and violent episodes have disrupted campus life in the latter half of the 1990s and early 2000s (Ruddell, Thomas, & Way, 2005). Scholars have described these as convivial and spontaneous events, occurring as beer riots or gatherings after the outcome of a campus sporting event; they are construed as issueless, without social organization, and absent of any instrumental purpose (McCarthy, Martin, & McPhail, 2005, 2007; Ruddell et al., 2005). Moreover, such issueless disruptions are an altogether different phenomenon than the collective action tactics being discussed in this chapter. Even so, McCarthy et al.'s (2007) work has demonstrated that the campus violence (and its reciprocal police response) is more likely to arise from these convivial campus gatherings than it is during college students' collective organizing efforts. Accordingly, campus community members should thus be careful to avoid conflating student mobilization tactics with campus-based convivial and spontaneous riot phenomena.

References

Altbach, P. G. (2006). Student politics: Activism and culture. In J. J. F. Forest & P. G. Altbach (Eds.), *International handbook of higher education* (pp. 329–345). Dordrecht, The Netherlands: Springer.

Altbach, P. G., & Cohen, R. (1990). American student activism: The post-sixties transformation. *Journal of Higher Education*, 61(1), 32–49.

American Council on Education. (1970). *Campus tensions: Analysis and recommendations. Report of the special committee on campus tensions*. Washington, DC: Author.

Apgar, S. (1995, September 5). Recent raids of sweatshops in California have illustrated a growing problem in major cities—The exploitation of a new wave of immigrant workers. Now federal regulators are asking retailers such as Dayton Hudson's Mervyn's to help solve the problem—Uncovering sweatshops. *Star Tribune: Newspaper of the Twin Cities*, p. 1D.

Astin, A. W., Astin, H. S., Bayer, A. E., & Bisconti, A. S. (1997). Overview of the unrest era. In L. F. Goodchild & H. S. Wechsler (Eds.), *The history of higher education* (2nd ed., pp. 724–738). Needham Heights, MA: Simon & Schuster.

Barnhardt, C. L. (2012). *Contemporary student activism: The educational contexts of socially-responsible student activism* (Unpublished doctoral dissertation). University of Michigan, Ann Arbor.

Benford, R. D., & Snow, D. A. (1992). Master frames and cycles of protest. In A. D. Morris & C. M. Mueller (Eds.), *Frontiers in social movement theory* (pp. 133–155). New Haven, CT: Yale University Press.

Bernstein, J. R. (2001). Right of expressive association and private universities' racial preferences and speech codes. *Williams & Mary Bill of Rights Journal, 9*, 619–643.

Binder, A., & Wood, K. (2012). *Becoming right: How campuses shape young conservatives.* Princeton, NJ: Princeton University Press.

Boren, M. E. (2001). *Student resistance: A history of an unruly subject.* New York, NY: Routledge.

Boris, E. (2002). Consumers of the world UNITE! Campaigns against sweating, past and present. In D. E. Bender & R. A. Greenwald (Eds.), *Sweatshop USA: The American sweatship in historical and global perspective* (pp. 203–224). New York, NY: Routledge.

Brennan, D. S. (2012, March 29). San Marcos: Occupy education protesters gather at Palomar College. *U-T San Diego.* Retrieved from http://www.utsandiego.com/news/2012/Mar/29/san-marcos-occupy-education-protestors-gather-at/

Bussian, J. R. (1995). Anatomy of the campus speech code: An examination of prevailing regulations. *Texas Law Review, 36*, 153–189.

Clark, B. R. (1972). The organizational saga in higher education. *Administrative Science Quarterly, 17*(2), 178–184.

Clemens, E. S. (2004). Organizational form as frame: Collective identity and political strategy in the American labor movement 1880–1920. In D. McAdam, J. D. McCarthy, & M. N. Zald (Eds.), *Comparative perspectives on social movements: Political opportunities, mobilizing structures, and cultural framings* (pp. 205–226). New York, NY: Cambridge University Press.

Collier, R. (1999, April 7). A movement at nation's schools to fight sweatshops/college logo apparel makes up big market. *San Francisco Chronicle.* Retrieved from http://www.sfgate.com/education/article/A-Movement-at-Nation-s-Schools-to-Fight-2935858.php

Cowan, R., Newton, N., Smith, J., Brozen, A., Burger, N., & Homstad, M. (1995). *Campus organizing guide for social justice groups.* Cambridge, MA: Center for Campus Organizing.

Davis, T. J. (2004). Assessing constitutional challenges to university free speech zones under Public Forum Doctrine. *Indiana Law Journal, 79*, 277–308.

Earl, J., Martin, A., McCarthy, J. D., & Soule, S. A. (2004). The use of newspaper data in the study of collective action. *Annual Reveiw of Sociology, 30*, 65–80.

Einwohner, R. L., & Spencer, J. W. (2005). That's how we do things here: Local culture and the construction of sweatshops and anti-sweatshop activism in two campus communities. *Sociologial Inquiry, 75*(2), 249–272.

Esbenshade, J. (2004). *Monitoring sweatshops: Workers, consumers, and the global apparel industry.* Philadelphia, PA: Temple University Press.

Featherstone, L. (2003). Students against sweatshops: A history. In D. E. Bender & R. A. Greenwald (Eds.), *Sweatshop USA: The American sweatshop in historical and global perspective* (pp. 247–264). New York, NY: Routledge.

Featherstone, L., & United Students Against Sweatshops. (2002). *Students against sweatshops.* New York, NY: Verso.

Gardner, L. (2013, January 29). Divesting from fossil-fuel companies is unlikely to harm endowments, report says. *The Chonicle of Higher Education.* Retrieved from http://chronicle.com/blogs/bottomline/divesting-in-fossil-fuels-shouldnt-harm-endowments-report-finds/

Goodwin, J., Jasper, J. M., & Polletta, F. (2004). Emotional dimensions of social movements. In D. A. Snow, S. A. Soule, & H. Kreisi (Eds.), *The Blackwell companion to social movements* (pp. 413–432). Malden, MA: Blackwell Publishing.

Gora, J. M., Goldberger, D., Stern, G., & Halperin, M. (1991). *The right to protest: The basic ACLU guide to free expression.* Carbondale: Southern Illinois University Press.

Hamrick, F. A. (1998). Democratic citizenship and student activism. *Journal of College Student Development, 39*(5), 449–460.

Harris, D. (1969). *Staff study of campus riots and disorders, October 1967–May 1969*. Prepared for the Permanent Subcommittee on Investigations of the Committee on Government Operations. Washington, DC: U.S. Government Printing Office.

Hirsch, E. L. (1999). Sacrifice for the cause: Group processess, recruitment, and commitment in a student social movement. In J. Freeman & V. Johnson (Eds.), *Waves of protest: Social movements since the sixties* (pp. 47–64). Lanham, MD: Rowman & Littlefield.

Hunter, D. E. (1988). Student activism: Growth through rebellion. In K. M. Miser (Ed.), *Student affairs and campus dissent* (pp. 23–40). Washington, DC: National Association of Student Personnel Administrators.

Jesse, D. (2012). Student protesters urge U-M regents to offer in-state tuition to undocumented residents. *Detroit Free Press*. Retrieved from http://www.freep.com/article/20121213/NEWS06/121213071/u-m-students-protest-tuition-undocumented-residents

Klandermans, B. (2004). The demand and supply of participation: Social-psychological correlates of participation in social movements. In D. A. Snow, S. A. Soule, & H. Kreisi (Eds.), *The Blackwell companion to social movements* (pp. 360–379). Malden, MA: Blackwell Publising.

Koopmans, R., & Rucht, D. (2002). Protest event analysis. In B. Klandermans & S. Staggenborg (Eds.), *Methods of social movement research: Social movements, protest, and contestation* (Vol. 16, pp. 231–259). Minneapolis: University of Minnesota Press.

Kuh, G., Schuh, J. H., Whitt, E. J., & Associates. (1991). *Involving colleges: Successful approaches to fostering student learning and personal development outside the classroom*. San Francisco, CA: Jossey-Bass.

Kurzman, C. (2008). Introduction—Meaning-making in social movements. *Anthropological Quarterly, 81*(1), 5–15.

McAdam, D. (1983). Tactical innovation and the pace of insurgency. *American Sociological Review, 48*, 735–754.

McCarthy, J. D., Martin, A. W., & McPhail, C. (2005, August). *Constraints on the freedom of public assembly: Police behavior and the demeanor of citizens in disorderly campus gatherings*. Paper presented at the 2005 Annual Meeting of the American Sociological Association, Philadelphia, PA.

McCarthy, J. D., Martin, A. W., & McPhail, C. (2007). Policing disorderly campus protests and convivial gatherings: The interaction of threat, social organization, and First Amendment guarantees. *Social Problems, 54*(3), 274–296.

McCarthy, J. D., & Zald, M. N. (1987). Resource mobilization and social movements. In M. N. Zald & J. D. McCarthy (Eds.), *Social movements in an organizational society* (pp. 15–47). New Brunswick, NJ: Transaction Books.

Meyer, D. S., & Tarrow, S. (1998). *The social movement society: Contentious politics for a new century*. Boulder, CO: Rowman & Littlefield.

Mueller, C. M. (1992). Building social movement theory. In A. D. Morris & C. M. Mueller (Eds.), *Frontiers in social movement theory* (pp. 3–26). New Haven, CT: Yale University Press.

Oliver, P. E., & Marwell, G. (1988). The paradox of group size in collective action: A theory of the critical mass. II. *American Sociological Review, 53*(1), 1–8.

Ramer, H. (2013, April 24). Dartmouth College cancels classes after protest. *Diverse Issues in Higher Education*. Retrieved from http://diverseeducation.com/article/52894/

Rhoads, R. A. (1998). *Freedom's web*. Baltimore, MD: Johns Hopkins University Press.

Rhoads, R. A., & Rhoades, G. (2005). Graduate employee unionization as symbol of and challenge to the corporatization of U.S. research universities. *Journal of Higher Education, 76*(3), 243–275.

Ross, A. (2003). The rise of the second anti-sweatshop movement. In D. E. Bender & R. A. Greenwald (Eds.), *Sweatshop USA* (pp. 225–246). New York, NY: Routledge.

Ross, R. J. S. (2004). *Slaves to fashion*. Ann Arbor: University of Michigan Press.

Ruddell, R., Thomas, M. O., & Way, L. B. (2005). Breaking the chain: Confronting issueless college town disturbances and riots. *Journal of Criminal Justice, 33*, 549–560.

Saucier, R. M. (1998, November 10). Sweatshop pact upset activists. White House task force produces deal on workers. *Bangor Daily News*.

Scranton, W. W. (1970). *The report of the President's commission on campus unrest*. Washington, DC: U.S. Government Printing Office.

Smith, J. (2001). Globalizing resistance: The battle of Seattle and the future of social movements. *Mobilization, 6*(1), 1–20.

Smith, R. B. (1993). The rise of the conservative student press. *Change, 25*(1), 24–29.

Soule, S. A. (1997). The student divestment movement in the United States and tactical diffusion: The shantytown protest. *Social Forces, 75*(3), 855–883.

Soule, S. A., & Earl, J. (2005). A movement society evaluated: Collective protest in the U.S. 1960–1986. *Mobilization, 10*(3), 345–364.

Stefancic, J., & Delgado, R. (1996). *No mercy: How conservative think tanks and foundations changed America's social agenda*. Philadelphia, PA: Temple University Press.

Tarrow, S. (1998). *Power in movement: Social movements and contentious politics*. New York, NY: Cambridge University Press.

Tilly, C. (2004). *Social movements 1768–2004*. Boulder, CO: Paradigm.

Walker, E. T., Martin, A. W., & McCarthy, J. D. (2008). Confronting the state, the corporation, and the academy: The influence of institutional targets on social movement repertoires. *American Journal of Sociology, 114*(1), 35–76.

Zald, M. N. (1996). Culture, ideology, and strategic framing. In D. McAdam, J. D. McCarthy, & M. N. Zald (Eds.), *Comparative perspectives on social movements: Political opportunities, mobilizing structures, and cultural framings* (pp. 261–274). Cambridge, UK: Cambridge University Press.

Zald, M. N., & Berger, M. A. (1978). Social movements in organizations—Coup d'etat, insurgency, and mass movements. *American Journal of Sociology, 83*(4), 823–861.

CASSIE L. BARNHARDT is an assistant professor in the Department of Educational Policy and Leadership Studies at the University of Iowa's College of Education.

NEW DIRECTIONS FOR HIGHER EDUCATION • DOI: 10.1002/he

5

This chapter explores the various performances of activism by students through sound, silence, gender, and dis/ability and how these performances connect to social change efforts around issues such as human trafficking, homeless children, hunger, and children with varying abilities.

Performances of Student Activism: Sound, Silence, Gender, and Dis/ability

Penny A. Pasque, Juanita Gamez Vargas

Activism has played a part in higher education for years, although performances of activism and resistance have looked different over the centuries as outlined in Christopher J. Broadhurst's chapter in this volume. It was the violent revolts of the late 18th and early 19th centuries ignited by wealthy undergraduates that helped create the early image of collegiate life (Horowitz, 1987). For example, during the early 1800s, Harvard students blew up buildings while students at Yale celebrated the Christmas season by breaking windows (Sorey & Gregory, 2010). During the same time period, students at Princeton University initiated revolts by firing pistols, crashing brickbats against walls and doors, taking over the administration building, smashing windows, and arming themselves against villagers in order to show discontent. It was University of North Carolina students who horsewhipped their president, stoned two professors, and threatened other faculty whereas Yale students bombed a residence hall in 1820 over the antiquated curriculum (Horowitz, 1987). College presidents and faculty of the day were determined to suppress such violent behavior and encouraged students to turn toward more covert forms of expression such as Greek organizations, which, interestingly, appealed to administrators *and* students because they "captured and preserved the spirit of the revolts" in a more docile fashion (Horowitz, 1987, p. 29).

In the 1960s, protest and activism surrounding the Vietnam War and racial injustice in the United States changed the consciousness of both students and faculty who participated as well as those who observed (Altbach,

The authors would like to thank Michael Horn, graduate assistant at the University of Oklahoma, for his assistance with this chapter.

NEW DIRECTIONS FOR HIGHER EDUCATION, no. 167, Fall 2014 © 2014 Wiley Periodicals, Inc.
Published online in Wiley Online Library (wileyonlinelibrary.com) • DOI: 10.1002/he.20105

1968, 1970; Geiger, 1999; Horowitz, 1987; Sorey & Gregory, 2010). For example, on October 1, 1964, as a part of the Berkeley Free Speech Movement, University of California, Berkeley students peacefully seized a police car and hundreds of students, faculty, administrators, and community members surrounded the car for hours (Sorey & Gregory, 2010); an open microphone was placed on top of the car, and anyone could sign up to speak for three minutes about his/her/hir[1] perspectives. One of the students who spoke was Mario Savio, who would later become the leader of the Free Speech Movement. Notably, the students were very careful about the car; they removed their shoes before climbing on it. First, they spoke from the hood and later from the roof. This was a moment for students to shift from watching the news to performatively participating through peaceful physical and verbal action on their home campus.

In a nonpeaceful example, the killing of students at Kent State University and Jackson State College in May 1970 evoked an outpouring of protest that was unmatched in earlier years (Horowitz, 1987). The visual image in a Pulitzer prize–winning photograph (by John Filo) of Mary Ann Vecchio at Kent State University kneeling in anguish over the body of Jeffrey Miller just after he was shot and killed by the Ohio National Guard is a photographic representation, or historical snapshot, of the escalation of activism and disaster that stays with us to this day. On the national level, the Scranton Commission established by President Nixon believed that students had provoked the majority of violent responses of the era; however, the report found that student deaths were more common than the deaths of their adversaries (President's Commission on Campus Unrest, 1970; also see Sorey & Gregory, 2010). Blame was not one-sided.

Activism and student resistance have been on the rise since the early 1990s and, according to scholars, have had positive effects on college and university students (Pascarella & Terenzini, 2005; Rhoads, 1998). Modern-day activism often utilizes technology (Biddix, 2010) and focuses on multiculturalism and social identity (Rhoads, 2000), including student efforts to increase racial diversity on campus (Vega, 2014; Woodhouse, 2014); gender inequity and reproductive rights (Allan, 2011; Revilla, 2002); the tragedy of September 11, 2001, in the United States and the wars around the world that followed (Sorey & Gregory, 2010; Woodward & Komives, 2003); anticorporatization (Dominguez, 2009) and financial retrenchment such as the international Occupy movement (which began on September 17, 2011); and education, such as the Day of Action to Defend Public Education on March 4, 2010, throughout the University of California and California State higher education systems (Hamedy, 2010; "In student protests," 2010; Rivera, Santa Cruz, & Gordon, 2010; Satyanarayana & Squires, 2010).

Each of these examples conveys a strong image of student performances of activism. Such performances of activism are a physical manifestation of resistance to marginalization and oppression in which students join together and speak out with their voices and bodies. Such student activism has been shown to lead to positive community development skills and cognitive development (Ollis, 2011). Current research has also found that students need to perceive the campus environment as safe in order to engage in activism and confront marginalization (Linder & Rodriguez, 2012; Revilla, 2012; Taines, 2012). Such safe spaces are also linked to retention and a more engaged student population (Taines, 2012). As the research shows, there are positive benefits to students and communities when they are engaged in activism, and college and university administrators have, hopefully, moved beyond the time period of perceiving student activism as negative and a place for blame.

Student Activism Through Academic Service Learning

This chapter explores the performances of activism physically and spatially embodied by students in a credit course that sought to create safe spaces for students to meaningfully explore the sociopolitical, cultural, and historical complexities of oppression as they engaged in community–university partnerships focused on social justice. The course intentionally included a service-learning component as a "text" for study, and students worked with one of the six area agencies that focused on education for homeless children, human trafficking, food distribution, home renovation for seniors, family clothing and supplies, and children with disabilities. Our hope is that this chapter will be instructive for faculty, administrators, and students interested in fostering activism and student development through curricular or cocurricular student-perceived safe spaces that focus on community–university collaboration and social justice.

Research Design.   This study engaged multistage methodologies and analytic processes in qualitative research as qualitative research is often iterative and unpredictable. (For additional examples of multistage qualitative research articles, see Haney, Thomas, & Vaughn [2011] and Leichtentritt & Rettig [2001].) Originally, critical discourse analysis (CDA) was the methodology utilized as a way to explore the discursive stories and experiences expressed by students engaged in a service-learning course (Ozias & Pasque, 2012). Specifically, CDA is a way of studying "how language figures in social processes" (Fairclough, 2001, p. 229)—in this case the social processes of community–university engagement in a graduate course. However, what emerged from the discourses included performances of student activism that seemed imperative to explore in more detail through this research study.

We draw from Koro-Ljungberg's (2012) "Methodology Is Movement Is Methodology" in which she argues against traditional linear designs for critical qualitative research. Koro-Ljungberg supports the recognition of "surprise" in order for social justice researchers to follow through on promises of addressing inequity and ways to translate this into methodological action (p. 83). In our case, this nonlinear design also helped us explore pedagogical choices and recommend changes in teaching and learning environments to foster student activism, which has positive impacts on students (Pascarella & Terenzini, 2005; Rhoads, 1998). In order to further explore these surprises, we turned to performance ethnography as a way to dive deeper into the performances we uncovered in the findings and make a stronger contribution regarding our understanding of student activism in service-learning and social justice courses.

As Denzin (2003) notes, performances are located in their historical moment and can take several forms including dramatic texts, poems, spoken word, natural texts, dramatic staged, or ethnodramas. Performances are interpretive events embedded in language. The natural text from this study (including student presentations, experiences in the local community engaging with people and geographic space within service-learning opportunities, ethnographic field notes, final papers, and capstone interviews) all contained performances of activism—or the retelling of performances of activism—from student engagement with community partners. Such performances "provide the grounds for liberation practice by opening up concrete situations that are being transformed through acts of resistance. In this way, performance ethnography advances the causes of liberation" (Denzin, 2003, p. 229). As such, this research intends to add to our knowledge about ways that inviting performances of activism and resistance in teaching and learning spaces may be beneficial in transforming students, community partners, the academy, and society.

Course Design.   The participants of this study were graduate students at a research-intensive university in a south central state who elected to take the course "Community–University Engagement toward Social Justice." This course was cosponsored by a department of higher education, center for social justice, and center for teaching, learning, and writing. The course included a textbook, *Service-Learning and Social Justice: Engaging Students in Social Change* (Cipolle, 2010), and a coursepack with selected journal articles and book chapters. The instructor gave students question prompts to use for weekly reflective online journals (or "blogs" as the students referred to them). The online journals were public, and students could respond or comment on each other's journals (unless a student chose to turn the journal in privately to the instructor). The questions were derived from various research sources on scaffolding student learning in service-learning courses (e.g., Fitzgerald, Burack, & Siefer, 2010a, 2010b; Jacoby, 1996; Quaye, 2005). A local community activist and PhD candidate served as a guest speaker and spoke on the topic of activism. Finally, as mentioned previously, the course intentionally included a service-learning component as a "text" for study within the course, and students could select one of six agencies that focused on education for homeless children, human trafficking, food distribution, home renovation for seniors, family clothing and supplies, and children with disabilities.

Participants and Data Set.   Fourteen of the 17 students in the course were enrolled in the higher education program concentrated on student affairs and were simultaneously employed in the field of student affairs on different campuses in the area. Two were sociology graduate students, and one was in the process of applying to a doctoral program. Notably, the students could opt in or out of participation in any aspect specific to the research study, and the professor (one of the authors) would not know if the students agreed to participate or not until after final grades were turned in, which added to the validity of the study (in other words, grades were not determined based on participation in the study).

The full data set generated by the students included online reflective journal entries, final papers, transcripts of interviews, a demographic survey with both short-answer and open-ended demographic questions, ethnographic field notes written by the faculty member, and field notes from phone interviews with community partners at the end of the course inquiring about the partners' experience with the course.

Performances of Student Activism

There were a number of performances of activism that emerged from the student experiences in which "the performative becomes an act of doing, an act of resistance, a way of connecting the biographical, the pedagogical, and the political" (Denzin, 2003, p. 14). In this section, we reflect upon a few examples of performances of activism juxtaposing sound (music) with silence and gender with dis/ability in order to deepen our understandings of the ways in which performance emerged directly from the students in this course and touched the lives of students and the community partners.

Performances of Activism: Sound and Silence.   A number of students created final capstone presentations that were both informative (including statistics, legislation, research, and reflective stories) and creative (including photographs, graphs, original artwork, and Prezis, which are visual presentations). While they were important contributions to learning, the capstone presentations were not identified as "performances of activism" for the purposes of this study. A few of the student presentations were quite unique in that they went beyond the traditional presentation and reflected several of the seven features of arts-based research as described by Barone and Eisner (1997) such as the presence of ambiguity, the use of capitalized and vernacular language, the promotion of empathy, the personal signature of the researcher/writer, and the presence of aesthetic form (also see Leavy, 2013).

For example, Ella (pseudonyms are used throughout the study) wove the lyrics of the song "Dare You To Move" by her favorite alternative rock band, Switchfoot, throughout the presentation that served as a capstone to her coursework.

Welcome to the fallout

Welcome to resistance

The tension is here

The tension is here... (Switchfoot, 2004)

As she played the music and shared each lyric with evocative photographs on the screen behind her, she related the powerful words to her experience with her community partner, an organization that serves thousands of people in the local area by providing a place for families recovering from a disaster, such as fire, tornado, or loss of home, and clothing, household items, and gifts for family members. The organization provides these gifts, which the families could not otherwise afford, for a one-dollar donation. Ella also wove the words of the song throughout her final paper as she reflected on the local policy, statistics, people, and experiential knowledge she had gained through the course and how she could actualize this awareness in her personal and professional life. This creative approach in the presentation and final paper provided an opportunity for Ella to share the depth of her knowledge about her community partner, the community members affiliated with this service site, her own experiences (past, present, and future), as well as to connect with the audience in a way that caused deep reflection for all involved.

In another example, Martha dimmed the lights for her research presentation that introduced the students in the course to the historical, economic, policy, and sociopolitical environment surrounding her service site. Martha, a Muslim student who wore a hajib to class on a regular basis, arrived in the front of class wearing a formal black burka and a large piece of silver duct tape over her mouth. Behind her motionless upright body flashed photographs (flash) and statistics (flash) of the women enslaved in human trafficking rings in the United States (flash) and around the globe (flash) for whom her service organization worked to raise awareness and funds. The silence in the background intensified as the eyes of the enslaved women were contrasted with Martha's own eyes—women silenced in different and multiple ways by oppressive systems of patriarchy, capitalism, and religious oppression.

In her work on performance ethnography, Madison (2012) describes performance interventions based on the work of Dwight Conquergood, an ethnographer and professor of performance studies, who stated that "to attend to the performances of symbolic bodily practices is a radically democratic endeavor, because the body expresses itself writ large everywhere" (p. 185). Further, people know experiences through the body where "coevalness" (p. 185) or the temporarily shared experiences of bodies in time actually *feel* a performance; in this way, all people in the audience and the performers actually feel the performance together—in the moment. This physical and radical encounter between Martha, the students, and the faculty member was that of an embodied experience of information, power, privilege, gender inequity, abuse, lived experience, and resistance. In this way, Martha required the audience to live the inequities present in her service site as she silently compelled us to see the parallels between their silenced voices and her own as a Muslim woman and as a volunteer whose voice could not eradicate human trafficking.

Martha identified with the women served by the organization as was evidenced through the choices she made in her performance during the final presentation. In addition, when asked in the survey, "Did the people served at your community partner site match many of/most of your social identities?" Martha answered "yes" and stated in her final paper, "I do not identify with the same religious affiliation as my partner site." The answers in the survey and final paper are not necessarily in conflict with each other; the complexities of identity here are important. While Martha did not identify with the same religious affiliation as her partner site (known to her upon selection of the site), she did identify with "many of/most of" its social identities. It could be that the deep connection between Martha and the women of her site may have allowed her to interrogate the structures of oppression in a profoundly meaningful manner. This connection may also have served as an impetus for her performance of activism that reflected on oppression across identities that are similar and different (e.g., gender, age, religion), silence, and structures that maintain violence and injustice.

In any case, we are reminded of the research by Linder and Rodriguez (2012) and Revilla (2012) that stressed the importance of safe spaces for activism in educational institutions where students often feel marginalized— safe space as defined by the students themselves, which may or may not reflect the instructor's definition of safe space. To be sure, it is important to create a space where students feel that they can engage in performances of activism, which are physical manifestations of resistance to marginalization and oppression in which people speak out with voices and bodies.

Performances of Activism: Gender and Dis/ability.   A number of graduate students reflected directly on their social identities (e.g., ability, age, ethnicity, gender, nationality, race, religion, sexual orientation, physical size) as they were included as an intentional aspect of the curriculum (Adams et al., 2010). It is important to note that some students abandoned discussions of identity later in the course whereas other students continued to reflect on their own identities and how these identities reflected privilege and/or oppression in relation to the community service sites. Further still, some students wrote about the physical manifestations of social identity as it pushed against dominant ways of knowing and being in society. This led to performances of activism and resistance within the community service site itself. Stated another way, these performances occurred in the local community service site (not the traditional brick and mortar classroom space), were performative in nature, and had a direct impact on the lives of community partners and graduate students. We focus here on two performances of activism—one of gender and one of dis/ability.

In the first example, Peter's performance of gender as a volunteer with a school for homeless children was a way of providing alternative representations of masculinity for young people and, in this way, served as a performance of activism and resistance against the norm. Peter shared his struggles in his final paper,

> Going into the service-learning experience, I was conscious of many social identities that I own. I self-present and identify as a white male. I am not oriented to relationships with either gender but have experienced emotional attraction to both sexes. I am a rural American and I started life in a lower income family that became a lower middle-income family. I experience depression and anxiety, I am obese, and I believe in God and classify myself as Christian. Throughout the service-learning experience, my most salient identity shifted in relation to the experience, and I became aware of identities that emerged in relation to the community partner members.
>
> Within the community partner site, I felt that I initially struggled most with my male identity. I believe that in this site there are definite beliefs about what masculinity looks like. During my first day of service, I was told the male students needed good role models and "guys to hang out and play basketball with them," the idea being that these male students may not have any other positive male role models in their lives. This simple statement seemed to confirm my worst fears about the service-learning site. I had worried that I would not measure up to the standard of being a male role model. While I identify as a man, the whole of my existence I have been reminded, overtly and covertly, that I am not manly. As such, I was worried that I would be ostracized by the students, like I was when I was their age, or by the site administrators if I was perceived as being not engaging. Not only was I fearful that I would be made fun of because of my voice and mannerisms, but also that I would not know what to do if I was asked to play basketball or football as I never participated in those activities as a child, and so as an adult I am unable to navigate those undertakings.

Peter reflected on his "worst fears" or the ways in which he does not conform to the traditional notions of being a good male role model for young boys as expected by the adults and children at the site. Yet, male identity and development are complex, masculinity is multidimensional, and gender identity interconnects with other aspects of a person's identity (Laker & Davis, 2011) as is reflected in Peter's description of himself and the ways in which he performed notions of gender and masculinity in this community service site.

As Tatum (2000) points out, dissonance is an important part of self-reflection and growth; the absence of it escapes our attention. For Peter, there was dissonance regarding his performances of identity; however, there may or may not have been dissonance for the administrators and young children at the community service site. Further, it is important to have an array of expansive performances of gender in our role models on and off campus in order to eradicate pervasive violence and create inclusive communities (see Adams et al., 2010).

It is also important for us to note Judith Butler's (1990) seminal work on gender performativity (the act of doing) and performance (that which is done) as well as Denzin's (2003) discussions of the ways in which these two (the doing and the done) have been blurred. In this case, we consider the performativities of gender in the moment that it occurred (as Peter served as a nondominant role model of masculinity), and, albeit not reflected in his own language, we argue that his presence represented marginalized perspectives of men and masculinity and may have had an impact on the lives of the children. In other words, Peter's presence at the community service site and his nontraditional "voice and mannerisms" were a role model for young people; he provided alternative performativities of gender. It was this performativity of gender that was the site of activism in the moment.

In a second example, Bryan's performance of activism was one that was also embodied, in this case, through his physical body within an inanimate wheelchair. First, the complexities of Bryan's social identities in his own words:

> As a person with a disability, I have often wondered how I could contribute to society. I have never been very mobile or quick because of my wheelchair. . . . I thought that because of my disability I would be very similar to the children at [community partner site for children with disabilities]. However, I quickly realized that my disability was one of the only things I have in common with the children at [the site] . . . Reflecting on my own social identities is not something I have done before this class . . . I am a 30-year-old, middle-class, straight, Christian, white male who happens to have cerebral palsy (CP). Of these identities, I would categorize myself as an agent for every social identity with the exception of disability. As I have gotten older, I realize that my social identities may matter more to some people than to myself. For instance, the fact that I was born with CP and use a wheelchair may make me a target because some people may be scared of those who are different from them. For the people who consider me a target, it is my responsibility to educate them about my disability and about others with disabilities. The class exercise and my experiences at [the site] were definitely eye-openers for me.

Bryan often wondered about his ability to "contribute to society" because of his disability. However, in the following example of a performance of activism, it is clear that Bryan not only contributed to society but also directly impacted the life of a young child at his site who was also in a wheelchair.

NEW DIRECTIONS FOR HIGHER EDUCATION • DOI: 10.1002/he

I spent most of my time reading with a little boy. While he struggled to speak, he was very intelligent and willing to sit down with me. I would ask him questions, and he would point and do his best to answer me verbally. It was easy to tell when he was excited to work with me because he would smile and laugh. He was very attentive. I got to work with him for a few weeks on Tuesdays and Thursdays, and while he had a really rough upbringing, he still possessed the joy of a child. [Two administrators at the site] told me that he never sat down to read. They told me he didn't like to read. [They] said I was the only one he would sit down and read with. Those comments filled my heart with joy. I also had the opportunity to help that little boy and other children with their homework. Despite tremendous obstacles, they did the best they could do and they did it with smiles on their faces.

For Bryan, the performance of activism was the act of rolling up in a wheelchair and working with a young boy, also in a wheelchair. The mirror of bodies in wheelchairs was a point of connection for this young boy and Bryan, despite other social identities that were not similar such as socioeconomic status and age (which Bryan describes in his final paper in more detail).

As Myers (2009) argues, it is important to move beyond current limitations in education to include various dis/abilities as we design curricula, programs, and services for accessibility for all students in a way that is both humanizing and inclusive. Bryan's experience reflected learning for himself *and* for the young person he worked with at the site. It was the embodied self within the confines of a wheelchair at a community partner site with children with disabilities that was the form of activism, and—for that activism—Bryan received positive responses in the form of smiles, laughter, and attention.

Discussion

In *Acts of Activism: Human Rights as Radical Performance*, Madison (2010) explained that it is the "small stories" of how human rights and social justice are fought that help us to locate radical performances that have the potential to explicate locations for social change. To be sure, the curricular performances of activism offered in this chapter are quite different from the Civil Rights Movements, Berkeley Free Speech Movement, the international Occupy movement, or activism experienced by the two authors. *These "small stories" are radical performances that emerged from community–university partnerships and shaped people's lives.* They are examples that extend beyond conventional notions of sound, silence, gender, and dis/ability in academic spaces as they represent and perform rituals from everyday life (Denzin, 2003) that ask each of us to work toward equity and social change.

We acknowledge that this course may have been selected because it fits into a student's schedule and that students may have learned from it—or not. However, for some students their performances of activism were displayed through sound or silence in capstone presentations and encouraged cognitive and affective learning by audience members. For other students, it was through performances of gender or dis/ability with young children that had the potential to make a difference for themselves and for the children. Again, each performance asks us—the audience members and readers—to learn, feel, and work toward social change.

Based on the unexpected surprises that emerged, we ask instructors and facilitators of curricular and cocurricular learning opportunities (including ourselves) these questions: In what ways are we constructing syllabi, community–university engagement programs, and service-learning events that foster safe spaces and invite performances of activism in order to deepen learning? In what ways are we creating spaces where students feel they can engage in performances of activism, which are physical manifestations of resistance to marginalization and oppression where people speak out with voices and bodies? We encourage faculty and administrators to work toward fostering student-defined and student-experienced safe space for exploration of social identities, participation with community service sites, and performances of activism toward social change, big or small.

Note

1. "Hir" and "ze" are commonly used pronouns that are inclusive of transgender and gender transgressive people in our communities and will be used throughout this chapter.

References

Adams, M., Blumenfeld, W. J., Castañeda, R., Hackman, H. W., Peters, M. L., & Zúñiga, Z. (2010). *Readings for diversity and social justice: An anthology on racism, antisemitism, sexism, heterosexism, ableism, and classism* (2nd ed.). New York, NY: Routledge.

Allan, E. J. (2011). *Women's status in higher education: Equity matters* [ASHE Higher Education Report, 37(1)]. San Francisco, CA: Jossey-Bass.

Altbach, P. (1968). *Turmoil and transition: Higher education and student politics in India.* New York, NY: Basic Books.

Altbach, P. (1970). Student movements in historical perspective: The Asian case. *Youth and Society, 1*, 333–357.

Barone, T., & Eisner, E. W. (1997). Arts-based educational research. In M. Jaeger (Ed.), *Complimentary methods for research in education* (2nd ed., pp. 73–116). Washington, DC: American Educational Research Association.

Biddix, J. P. (2010). Technology uses in campus activism from 2000 to 2008: Implications for civic learning. *Journal of College Student Development, 51*(6), 670–693.

Butler, J. (1990). *Gender trouble: Feminism and the subversion of identity.* New York, NY: Routledge.

Cipolle, S. B. (2010). *Service-learning and social justice: Engaging students in social change.* New York, NY: Rowman & Littlefield.

Denzin, N. K. (2003). *Performance ethnography: Critical pedagogy and the politics of culture.* Thousand Oaks, CA: Sage.

Dominguez, R. F. (2009). U.S. college student activism during an era of neoliberalism: A qualitative study of students against sweatshops. *The Australian Educational Researcher, 36*(3), 125–138.

Fairclough, N. (2001). The discourse of new labour: Critical discourse analysis. In M. Wetherell, S. Taylor, & S. J. Yates (Eds.), *Discourse as data: A guide for analysis* (pp. 229–266). Thousand Oaks, CA: Sage.

Fitzgerald, H. E., Burack, C., & Siefer, S. (Eds.). (2010a). *Handbook of engaged scholarship: Contemporary landscapes, future directions: Volume I: Institutional change*. East Lansing: Michigan State University Press.

Fitzgerald, H. E., Burack, C., & Siefer, S. (Eds.). (2010b). *Handbook of engaged scholarship: Contemporary landscapes, future directions: Volume II: Community–campus partnerships*. East Lansing: Michigan State University Press.

Geiger, R. (1999). The ten generations of American-higher education. In P. G. Altbach, R. O. Berdahl, & P. J. Gumport (Eds.), *American higher education in the twenty-first century: Social, political and economic challenges* (pp. 39–69). Baltimore, MD: Johns Hopkins University Press.

Hamedy, S. (2010, March 4). University of California students protest tuition hikes. *The Daily Free Press*. Retrieved from http://dailyfreepress.com/2010/03/04/university-of-california-students-protest-tuition-hikes/

Haney, K. G., Thomas, J., & Vaughn, C. (2011). Identity border crossings within school communities, precursors to restorative conferencing: A symbolic interactionist study. *The School Community Journal, 21*(2), 55–80.

Horowitz, H. L. (1987). *Campus life: Undergraduate cultures from the end of the eighteenth century to present*. Chicago, IL: University of Chicago Press.

In student protests, it's important to be peaceful [Editorial]. (2010, March 5). *The Marshall Parthenon*. Retrieved from http://www.marshallparthenon.com/opinion/in-student-protests-it-s-important-to-be-peaceful-1.2181355

Jacoby, B. (1996). *Service-learning in higher education: Concepts and practices*. San Francisco, CA: Jossey-Bass.

Koro-Ljungberg, M. (2012). Methodology is movement is methodology. In S. R. Steinberg & G. S. Cannella (Eds.), *Critical qualitative research reader* (pp. 82–90). New York, NY: Peter Lang.

Laker, J. A., & Davis, T. (Eds.). (2011). *Masculinities in higher education: Theoretical and practical considerations*. New York, NY: Routledge.

Leavy, P. (2013). *Fiction as research practice: Short stories, novellas, and novels*. Walnut Creek, CA: Left Coast Press.

Leichtentritt, R. D., & Rettig, K. D. (2001). The construction of the good death: A dramaturgy approach. *Journal of Aging Studies, 15*(1), 85–104.

Linder, C., & Rodriguez, K. L. (2012). Learning from the experiences of self-identified women of color activists. *Journal of College Student Development, 53*(3), 383–398.

Madison, D. S. (2010). *Acts of activism: Human rights as radical performance*. Cambridge, UK: Cambridge University Press.

Madison, D. S. (2012). *Critical ethnography: Method, ethics, and performance* (2nd ed.). Los Angeles, CA: Sage.

Myers, K. (2009). A new vision for disability education: Moving from the add-on. *About Campus, 14*(5), 15–21.

Ollis, T. (2011). Learning in social action: The informal and social learning dimension of circumstantial and lifelong activists. *Australian Journal of Adult Learning, 51*(2), 248–268.

Ozias, M., & Pasque, P. A. (2012, November). *Community-university partnerships toward social justice: A critical discourse analysis of student writing and talking*. Paper presented at the meeting of the Association for the Study of Higher Education, Las Vegas, NV.

Pascarella, E. T., & Terenzini, P. T. (2005). *How college affects students*. San Francisco, CA: Jossey-Bass.

President's Commission on Campus Unrest. (1970). *The report of the President's commission on campus unrest*. New York, NY: Arno Press.

Quaye, S. J. (2005). Let us speak: Including students' voices in the public good of higher education. In A. J. Kezar, T. C. Chambers, & J. Burkhardt (Eds.), *Higher education for the public good: Emerging voices from a national movement* (pp. 293–307). San Francisco, CA: Jossey-Bass.

Revilla, A. T. (2002). Activism. In A. M. M. Alemán & K. A. Renn (Eds.), *Women in higher education: An encyclopedia* (pp. 262–264). Santa Barbara, CA: ABC-Clio.

Revilla, A. T. (2012). What happens if Vegas does not stay in Vegas: Youth leadership in the immigrant rights movement in Las Vegas, 2006. *Aztlán: A Journal of Chicano Studies, 37*(1), 87–115.

Rhoads, R. (1998). Student protest and multicultural reform: Making sense of campus unrest in the 1990s. *Journal of Higher Education, 69*(6), 621–646.

Rhoads, R. (2000). *Freedom's web: Student activism in an age of cultural diversity*. Baltimore, MD: Johns Hopkins University Press.

Rivera, C., Santa Cruz, N., & Gordon, L. (2010, March 5). Thousands protest California education cuts. *Los Angeles Times*. Retrieved from http://articles.latimes.com/2010/mar/05/local/la-me-protests5-2010mar05

Satyanarayana, M., & Squires, J. (2010, March 5). *Student protest shuts down campus of UC Santa Cruz*. Retrieved from http://www.newsrecord.org/student-protest-shuts-down-campus-of-uc-santa-cruz/article_5901a1bc-baac-5a64-a87a-aa70caf1052f.html

Sorey, K. C., & Gregory, D. (2010). Protests in the sixties. *The College Student Affairs Journal, 28*(2), 184–206.

Switchfoot. (2004). Dare you to move. *Learning to Breathe*. J. Foreman (Writer), C. Peacock & J. Fields (Producers). Tampa, FL: Re:think Records.

Taines, C. (2012). Intervening in alienation: The outcomes for urban youth of participating in school activism. *American Educational Research Journal, 49*(1), 53–86.

Tatum, B. (2000). The complexity of identity: Who am I? In M. Adams, W. J. Blumenfeld, R. Castañeda, W. H. Hackman, M. L. Peters, & X. Zúñiga (Eds.), *Readings for diversity and social justice: An anthology on racism, antisemitism, sexism, heterosexism, ableism, and classism* (pp. 9–14). New York, NY: Routledge.

Vega, T. (2014, February 24). Colorblind notion aside, colleges grapple with racial tension. *New York Times*. Retrieved from http://www.nytimes.com/2014/02/25/us/colorblind-notion-aside-colleges-grapple-with-racial-tension.html

Woodhouse, K. (2014, February 19). 1,000-plus flock to University of Michigan "speak out" to share minority experience, support activism. *Ann Arbor News*. Retrieved from http://www.mlive.com/news/ann-arbor/index.ssf/2014/02/university_of_michigan_student_104.html

Woodward, W. B., & Komives, S. R. (2003). Shaping the future. In S. R. Komives, D. B. Woodard, Jr., & Associates (Eds.), *Student services: A handbook for the profession* (4th ed., pp. 637–655). San Francisco, CA: Jossey-Bass.

PENNY A. PASQUE *is an associate professor in the Department of Educational Leadership & Policy Studies and Women's & Gender Studies/Center for Social Justice at the University of Oklahoma.*

JUANITA GAMEZ VARGAS *is an assistant professor in the Adult & Higher Education Department of Educational Leadership & Policy Studies at the University of Oklahoma.*

This chapter traces two decades of published research on learning outcomes related to campus activism and reports results from a speculative study considering civic outcomes from participation in campus political and war demonstrations.

Development Through Dissent: Campus Activism as Civic Learning

J. Patrick Biddix

In 2009, Dey and Associates stressed the active role of secondary educators in producing an educated and engaged citizenry, advocating civic learning as an essential outcome for college students. Ardaiolo, Neilson, and Daugherty (2011) drew a parallel between this emphasis and *Learning Reconsidered*'s civic engagement learning outcome (Keeling & Associates, 2004), encouraging educators to foster and sustain campus-based civic learning opportunities. More recently in 2012, the U.S. Department of Education supported a partnership to create The National Task Force on Civic Learning and Democratic Engagement (hereafter The National Task Force), which produced *A Crucible Moment: College Learning and Democracy's Future* (2012), a call to action and report focusing on the need for realigning higher education with its historical democratic mission (Harper, 1905). Specifically, the authors articulated a fundamental need for higher education to produce engaged citizens.

Yet despite notable efforts, major empirical gaps in the research persist with regard to *how* specific activities actually affect civic and democratic learning outcomes (Carnegie Foundation for the Advancement of Teaching, 2006). For example, Colby, Ehrlich, Beaumont, and Stephens (2003), working with the Carnegie Foundation for the Advancement of Teaching, drew on results from a case study of 12 institutions to offer a framework for considering moral and civic development. The work served as an advocacy resource for educating campus administrators on the importance of civic engagement and offered valuable examples where none previously existed. Jacoby and Associates (2009) added recommendations for creating and supporting civic learning opportunities on campus, including a final chapter (Jacoby & Hollander, 2009) detailing institutional factors affecting civic learning. Further, much of the literature to date evaluating civic

NEW DIRECTIONS FOR HIGHER EDUCATION, no. 167, Fall 2014 © 2014 Wiley Periodicals, Inc.
Published online in Wiley Online Library (wileyonlinelibrary.com) • DOI: 10.1002/he.20106

outcomes from the college experience has focused on service learning or other apolitical forms of involvement (Finley, 2011). Butin (2012) suggested such activities were not enough "to truly fashion and create meaningful and long-lasting change both in our institutions and in our communities" (p. 1). To contextualize this view, this chapter highlights the criticism of service, reviews the research linking activism to learning outcomes, and offers an initial assessment using longitudinal data to evidence the inclusion of activism as a contributor to civic learning.

Service and Volunteerism as Apolitical Involvement

Kuh (2008) identified service learning as a high-impact practice having positive effects on student learning and retention. Characteristics of high-impact practices include the demand for considerable time and effort, a provision of cocurricular learning opportunities, facilitation of mindful interactions, encouragement of interactions with diverse others, and frequent and meaningful feedback. Researchers have demonstrated that participation in volunteerism and service experience increases awareness of social values (Astin & Sax, 1998); however, the outcome of these activities on effective participation in a democratic society may be questionable (Bryant, Gayles, & Davis, 2011). Lopez et al.'s (2006) findings from a national survey of 15- to 25-year-olds suggest that perhaps we should not be so quick to consider service a form of democratic engagement. The researchers found most young people viewed volunteering as simply a means of helping others and not as a way of addressing a social or political problem. Finley (2011, 2012), following an extensive review of research drawn from longitudinal data, noted that while community service and service learning were research-supported paths to civic learning, neither offered the ability to work with others *through differences* to solve public problems.

The authors of *A Crucible Moment* (The National Task Force, 2012) emphasized that community service, while a research-supported path to civic learning, was "not necessarily the same as democratic engagement with others across differences to collectively solve public problems" (p. 5). They advocated teaching students the value of collaborative and direct action to help students move from civic learning to civic action, "thus better preparing them to serve their communities and the nation as informed, active citizens when they graduate" (p. 8). Political theorist Benjamin Barber (1984) emphasized the need for a civic education in democratic responsibility as well as strong democratic practices. Later supporting this approach, Barber (2012) offered a characterization of democracy as conflict resolution—or finding ways for people to reconcile differences to live together. He wrote, "too many people think democracy is about consensus, whereas in reality it is about conflict and division. In the absence of division there is no need for democracy or for politics: we would live together in natural harmony" (p. 2).

Campus Activism as Civic Learning

Student development theorists in the 1990s (Astin, 1993; Chambers & Phelps, 1993; Hamrick, 1998; Rhoads, 1998) suggested participation in campus activism was developmental, rather than detrimental, to student learning. Building on these and similar studies, the authors of *Learning Reconsidered* (Keeling & Associates, 2004) urged educators to view activism as an expression of civic engagement, later described as offering developmental opportunities for students (Komives, Lucas, & McMahon, 2007). More recently, researchers (Biddix, 2010; Biddix, Somers, & Polman, 2009) qualitatively identified civic learning outcomes from participation in student activism (e.g., campus demonstrations) though no major quantitative study of participants and learning outcomes from participation during the 2000s has been undertaken to date. This initial exploratory study sought to address this deficiency using data from a nationally representative survey.

Hamrick (1998) used a case study approach to point out core principles of democracy in student unrest. Drawing on Gutmann's (1987) work, Hamrick named mobilizing others around a common cause, forming consensus among group members for activity, and fighting for an issue that affects the common good as enacted democratic practices. Hunter (1988) described activist participation as evidence of an emerging social consciousness, noting, "the activities of campus protest—rallies, debates, boycotts—provide college youth with opportunities for community and contexts for their exploration of personal growth" (p. 35). Chambers and Phelps (1993) drew similarities between leadership outcomes from activist participation and involvement in traditional organizations such as student government, fraternities, and clubs.

Biddix verified many of these proposed outcomes in his qualitative studies of activist participation. Working with Somers and Polman, he identified learning outcomes from participation in a living wage sit-in on a single campus (Biddix et al., 2009). In a study of activist women leaders, Biddix (2010) found similar practices to those described by Hamrick (1998) and Hunter (1988) enacted during several phases of activist participation. The lone other study drawing outcomes-based considerations from campus activism is Featherstone's (2002) book-length treatment of the Students Against Sweatshops Movement in the late 1990s and early 2000s. Rhoads's (1997, 1998) work offers further considerations, again taking a case study/phenomenological approach, at situating student actions in the boarder context of learning. More recently, Rhoads and Rhoades (2005) examined graduate student unionization using a similar approach.

Developmental outcomes from participation were a common, if not explicit, theme in each of the previously reviewed works. Common themes from the literature related to change and commitment to social involvement, awareness of issues, and self-confidence as related to advocacy for change. With one exception, Billings and Terkla's (2011) single-institution study of civic engagement and campus culture, qualitative methodologies were used to arrive at these considerations. Few studies have explored, quantitatively, the effects of various forms of civic engagement, especially student demonstration, on student outcomes. Reason, Cox, McIntosh, and Terenzini (2011) referred to direct and teachable forms of civic learning as "democratic action-taking," echoing Engle and Ochoa's (1988) and Gutmann's (1987) concept of active citizenship and invoking Barber's (1984, 2004) conception of direct action as form of citizenship training. A measure evaluating direct and/or teachable civic learning was not identifiable in existing data sets. The following preliminary study sought to introduce and evaluate a multifaceted, civic learning variable to stimulate evidence-based discussion and provide direction for future research.

Preliminary Empirical Evidence

This speculative study explored the effect of participation in campus demonstrations on three measures selected to approximate civic learning outcomes: social agency, civic awareness, and outspoken leadership. Social agency referred to changes in students' value of political and social involvement. Civic awareness referred to changes in students' understanding of issues in their community, nation, and world. Outspoken leadership referred to changes in students' self-relation of leadership, public speaking, risk taking, and social self-confidence. Data from the 2007 administration of the College Senior Survey (hereafter CSS 2007) were used to evaluate the research questions. The CSS, developed by the Higher Education Research Institute (HERI) at the University of California, Los Angeles (UCLA) and administered through the Cooperative Institutional Research Program (CIRP), focuses on a broad range of student experiences. The CSS is typically administered as an exit survey, and individual responses can be linked with The American Freshman Survey, also administered by UCLA's CIRP, to examine within-college effects as repeated measures.

After gaining access to the data set and receiving institutional review board approval, data screening began. Two issues had to be resolved prior to analysis: (a) 95% of cases in the data set came from private institutions; and (b) several cases had missing values on the covariate, factors, and outcomes measures. To address the former, the study was delimited to four-year private institutions. To address the latter, a missing-values analysis was conducted, which revealed data were missing completely at random. Since less than 5% of cases had missing data, listwise deletion proceeded. No other adjustments or transformations were needed to meet the statistical assumptions of procedures used in this study. The final data set consisted of 9,903 students attending 97 four-year private institutions.

Previously reviewed research suggested the most reliable predictor of participation in campus demonstrations was participation in high school demonstrations (Astin, Astin, Bayer, & Bisconti, 1975; Biddix, 2006). A

NEW DIRECTIONS FOR HIGHER EDUCATION • DOI: 10.1002/he

dummy coded variable from TFS 2003, participation in high school demonstrations, was used as an approximate control for the effect of previous experience. Statistically, this is accomplished by regressing the covariate on the dependent variables prior to the main analysis to adjust the outcome means (Tabachnick & Fidell, 2001). A factorial (3 × 3) MANCOVA model was hypothesized using precollege demonstration experience as a covariate, two factors for demonstration participation, and the three outcome measures. Participation in campus demonstrations was evaluated using two self-reported college experiences: (a) participated in political demonstrations and (b) demonstrated for/against a war. Both were scaled 1 to 3, with 1 indicating "not at all," 2 "some of the time," and 3 "frequently." Three research questions were posed:

1. Are there significant mean differences in civic learning among undergraduate participants in college *political demonstrations* after removing the effect of previous participation in demonstrations in high school?
2. Are there significant mean differences in civic learning among undergraduate participants in college *war demonstrations* after removing the effect of previous participation in demonstrations in high school?
3. Does undergraduate student participation in *political and war demonstrations* interact to affect the capacity for civic learning after removing the effect of previous participation in demonstrations in high school? If so, how do the types of demonstrations differ along those measures?

The three dependent factors—social agency, civic awareness, and outspoken leadership—were rescaled to a z-score metric (20–80 range) by multiplying individual scores by 10 then adding 50, which set the initial mean to 50 ($SD = 10$). HERI staff later updated social agency and civic awareness, so that the mean for social agency was 52.67 ($SD = 9.78$) and the mean for civic awareness was 52.16 ($SD = 8.29$). Outspoken leadership remained standardized.

Six questions derived from CSS 2007 comprised social agency, individually asking students to rate the importance they assigned to the following items: (a) keeping up to date with political affairs, (b) participating in a community action program, (c) influencing social values, (d) becoming a community leader, (e) helping others who are in difficulty, and (f) helping to promote racial understanding. Three questions derived from CSS 2007 comprised civic awareness, individually asking students to rate the importance they assigned to the following items: (a) understanding of national issues, (b) understanding of global issues, and (c) understanding of social problems facing your community.

Four questions derived from CSS 2007 comprised outspoken leadership, individually asking students to rate themselves on the following traits in relation to peers: (a) leadership ability, (b) public speaking ability, (c) risk taking, and (d) self-confidence (social). This factor was developed by the researcher using principal component factor analysis, with an oblique rotation (promax) as used in previous analyses of CSS/TFS matched data (Eagan, Herrera, Garibay, Hurtado, & Chang, 2011; Garcia & Hurtado, 2011). The Cronbach's alpha for this factor was 0.748. Individual items loaded as follows: leadership ability (0.772), public speaking ability (0.774), risk taking (0.765), and self-confidence (social) (0.710).

Results

Demographics of the sample showed 61.4% of participants were female and identified as White/Caucasian (83.1%), followed by Asian (5.1%), other/multiracial (5.1%), Latino (3.9%), and Black/African American (2.7%). Catholic was the largest religious preference (46.3%), followed by Protestant (33.9%), no preference (13.9%), other religion (3.1%), and Jewish (2.8%). Middle of the road was the majority political view (44.7%), with conservative (27.8%) and liberal (27.4%) nearly equally represented. The majority of students in the sample had not participated in demonstrations in high school (62.8%), while about a third had done so occasionally (29.4%), and a few frequently (8.0%). Institutional type was distributed consistently by basic Carnegie classification with baccalaureate (36.7%), master's (30.1%), and doctoral/research (33.2%). Selectivity was approximated using a combined SAT score recoded into percentiles. The largest group was moderately selective in the 50th (50.3%), followed by a group of very selective institutions in the 75th (26.8%), and selective in the 25th (22.9%). Full-time enrollment was defined as small institutions (2,499 or less students, 33.9%), mid-sized institutions (2,500–7,499 students, 44.2%), and large institutions (over 7,500, 21.9%).

Since large sample sizes can be more sensitive to Type I errors (Tabachnick & Fidell, 2001), alpha for all analyses was interpreted at $\alpha = 0.001$ or greater. Prior to the main analysis, the two types of demonstrations (political demonstrations and war demonstrations) were examined to confirm significant difference, since it was important to determine whether the two variables represented two distinctive experiences. A chi-square test revealed this difference, showing a strong association, as expected. Students equally did not participate in either type of demonstration (not at all/not at all = 92.0%), but only about half participated in both types some of the time (54.2%) and frequently (56.5%). Mixed participation (e.g., not at all/frequently) was considerably less related.

A factorial (3 × 3) MANCOVA model examined potential main and interaction effects for protest type and frequency on the hypothesized three-part dependent variable. The covariate, participation in demonstrations in high school, significantly influenced the combined dependent variable. Univariate ANOVA results indicated significance for only two of the dependent factors, social agency and outspoken leadership, which led to statistical

Figure 6.1. Main Effects for Participation in Demonstration by Type and Frequency

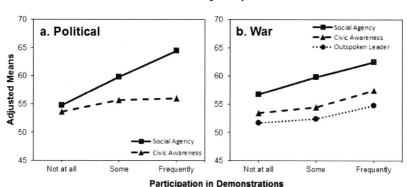

adjustments to means. The main effect of political demonstration significantly influenced the combined dependent variable. Univariate ANOVA results indicated significance for only two of the dependent factors: social agency and civic awareness. As shown in Figure 6.1(a), participation in political demonstrations led to the most pronounced and consistent gain in social agency score. Students who participated in political demonstrations some of the time averaged a 4.95-point gain over those who did not participate at all; students who frequently participated averaged an additional 4.64-point gain. Changes in civic awareness among political demonstrations were less dramatic, from not at all to some of the time (+2.14), and barely increased from some of the time to frequently (+0.29).

The main effect of war demonstration significantly influenced the combined dependent variable. Univariate ANOVA results indicated significance for all three of the dependent factors—social agency, civic awareness, and outspoken leadership—which led to statistical adjustments to means. As shown in Figure 6.1(b), participation in war demonstrations led to less pronounced, but more comprehensive changes that included all three aspects of civic learning. Students who participated in war demonstrations some of the time averaged a 3.09-point gain in social agency over those who did not participate at all; students who frequently participated averaged an additional 2.77-point gain. Changes in civic awareness were more dramatic for frequent participants over those who participated some of the time (+2.99), than for some of the time participants over those who did not participate at all (+1.07). Students who participated in war demonstrations also showed changes on outspoken leadership. Only a small increase resulted from not at all to some of the time (+0.75) while a more pronounced additional gain could be seen for those who participated frequently (+2.36).

Differences in capacity for civic learning by political and war demonstration frequency, controlling for previous demonstration experiences in

Figure 6.2. Interaction Effects for Participation in Demonstration by Combined Type and Frequency

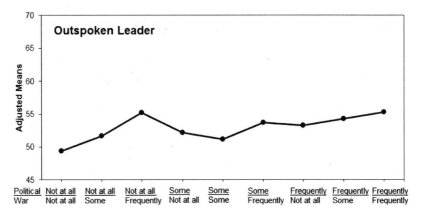

high school, were examined across three dimensions: social agency, civic awareness, and outspoken leadership. The interaction effect of political and war demonstration indicated a significant effect on the combined dependent variable. Univariate ANOVA results indicated significance for only one of the dependent factors, outspoken leadership. Figure 6.2 displays those results.

Students who participated in only war demonstrations some of the time averaged a 2.21-point gain over students who did not participate in either type of demonstration. This gain rose additional 3.56-points for frequent war-only demonstration participants. Students who were participants in political demonstrations some of the time and did not participate in war demonstrations experienced the only negative gain (−1.03); participating some of the time in both types of demonstration led to an expected increase (+2.53). Students who frequently participated in political demonstrations, but only participated in war demonstrations some of the time saw a marginal gain (+1.07) over those who did not participate in war demonstrations. A surprisingly low gain resulted from frequently participating in political and some of the time in war to frequently participating on both types of demonstrations (+1.00).

Summary Findings

Overall, findings from this study suggest that despite a striking overall effect for political demonstration on social agency, participation in war demonstration was the most closely related to the hypothesized measure of civic learning. Students who participated more frequently experienced consistent gains in social agency (action), civic awareness (knowledge), and outspoken leadership (skills) than those who participated in political demonstration or a combination of the two. The main and interaction effect produced by war demonstration on outspoken leadership suggests that either the experience or factors not measured in this study but associated with the activity are more related to skills associated with taking action. Several possibilities may account for this mixed interaction effect. As previously noted, political demonstration did not affect outspoken leadership, but the effect for war was strong enough to create a significant interaction effect. The negative and otherwise marginal changes in outspoken leadership shown in Figure 6.2 occur for pairs with the same or higher political participation than war. This suggests a suppressor effect for political demonstration frequency on war demonstration. In other words, the positive effect war demonstration creates with regard to outspoken leadership are mediated when students also participate in political demonstrations.

Discussion and Considerations

The National Task Force (2012) advocated for shared responsibility among faculty, student affairs professionals, and administrators to accomplish central work of advancing civic learning and democratic engagement. The first recommendation was to "foster a civic ethos across all parts of campus and educational culture" and was defined under the first bullet point as "establish[ing] a commitment to public-mindedness and a concern for the well-being of others as defining institutional characteristics, and explicitly articulat[ing] that commitment via consequential public document and speeches" (p. 31). In describing the learning environment, The National Task Force (2012) rhetorically asked, what would a civic-minded campus look like? As we work to define and understand how civic learning might be accomplished, it is important to identify, operationalize, and evaluate potential capacity builders among college experiences beyond service and curricular settings (Finley, 2012). Understanding how extracurricular activities contribute to civic learning is essential for educators and educational policy makers charged with creating, fostering, and sustaining a robust learning environment (The National Task Force, 2012).

Research has shown students can be exposed to civic learning in multiple ways (Finley, 2011), yet few researchers have empirically evaluated activities beyond service and volunteerism. Finley (2012), in a document summarizing contemporary research on student civic learning gains informing *A Crucible Moment*, identified consistent four-year gains for in-college civic knowledge and engagement on multiple dimensions within the CIRP, National Study of Student Engagement, and Wabash Study findings. Based on these findings, Finley recommended additional research to incorporate multiple measures of civic competencies beyond self-reported gains, experiences of underserved students, outcomes more closely related to civic capacity building, evidence related to global knowledge and skills, and the need for greater evidence on variations in civic learning impact measures of student success. Prior to the present study, a lack of cross-institutional, longitudinal findings to support these considerations limited more generalizable inferences.

As previous qualitative studies have noted, participating in campus demonstrations can positively affect civic learning outcomes (Biddix et al., 2009; Hamrick, 1998). The present study revealed that participating in demonstrations can uniquely and positively affect students' value of political and social involvement, making the case for dissent as a means of fostering the development of civically minded "responsible global and local citizens" (Dey & Associates, 2009, p. 1) who value active democratic engagement (Engle & Ochoa, 1988; Gutmann, 1987). These findings do not suggest educators should incite campus rebellion, but indicate they should work to ensure that campus conditions invite and tolerate opposing viewpoints and actions (Goldfinger, 2009; Misa, Anderson, & Yamamura, 2005; Sax, 2000; Strayhorn, 2005). Educators charged with "creating conditions that matter" (Kuh, Kinzie, Schuh, & Whitt, 2005) should examine current policies and precedent regarding campus expression, recognizing the positive outcomes campus demonstration may yield for both the participants and the larger campus community. Specifically, Ardaiolo et al. (2011), citing *Learning Reconsidered's* civic engagement learning outcome (Keeling & Associates, 2004), strengthened this consideration by identifying the articulated role of student affairs practitioners in fostering and sustaining a campus climate for civic learning.

One strategy Jacoby and Hollander (2009) offered for cultivating and sustaining campus civic engagement was to provide access and opportunity for students to participate in a variety of activities. Research assessing the effect of campus environments on civic learning conditions has suggested the value of this approach. Sax (2000), using a large-scale data set, discovered a peer effect among noninvolved students who perceived their campus as accepting of expression. This valuing of campus expression not only promotes civic learning among participants (supported by findings in this study), but also may lead to more civic-mindedness among peers. In a single-campus study of 435 students, Nishishiba, Nelson, and Shinn (2005) found community efficacy to be among the strongest predictors for direct action, or the extent to which a student would participate in a protest or boycott for an issue of concern. Community efficacy was a construct variable partially defined as perception about community as a change agent and belief in a capacity for coming together. Using longitudinal measures, Bryant et al. (2011) found that a college culture that values the goal of social activism and related cocurricular involvement facilitates adoption of social and political concerns. This finding empirically supported Seider's (2007) notion that civic-minded values and behaviors must be internalized for actions to "catalyze." A critical step in understanding how activities such as demonstrations affect both participants and the larger learning environment is to build understanding of how actions affect outcomes through continued research. Further, educators should incorporate forms of student activism as potential learning activities when assessing civic engagement measures and outcomes.

Several provocative questions directly related to demonstration participation were left unanswered by this study, due to the measurement of the experiences. For example, what is "some of the time" versus "frequent" involvement in demonstrations? Do students view and report this measure quantitatively differently? Research on student responses to this type of measure scale is mixed (McCormick & McClenney, 2012; Porter, 2009); therefore, studies are needed to differentiate the degree of involvement or engagement to understand more precisely the effect of participating in demonstrations. Further, does war demonstration mean "the war" or "a war?" Is it differently interpreted? Does war mean a conflict involving the United States that is specifically defined? Political demonstration perhaps is even more ambiguous. For example, is such participation in protest of a campus policy, against the visit of a controversial campus speaker, or related to a current local, state, or national issue? These additional considerations suggest the need for follow-up qualitative research to describe "participation" and to explore variation within the two types of demonstration as well as to identify associated activities. Such research can add a level preciseness and clarity unachievable with the presently available data and perhaps lead to a better understanding of what civic learning is, how campus activism affects it, and to what degree educators can support students who participate.

References

Ardaiolo, F. P., Neilson, S., & Daugherty, T. K. (2011). Teaching students personal and social responsibility with measurable learning outcomes. *Journal of College & Character, 12*(2), 1–9.

Astin, A. W. (1993). *What matters in college? Four critical years revisited.* San Francisco, CA: Jossey-Bass.

Astin, A. W., Astin, H. S., Bayer, A. E., & Bisconti, A. S. (1975). *The power of protest.* San Francisco, CA: Jossey-Bass.

Astin, A. W., & Sax, L. J. (1998). How undergraduates are affected by service participation. *Journal of College Student Development, 39*(3), 251–263.

Barber, B. R. (1984). *Strong democracy: Participatory politics for a new age.* Los Angeles: University of California Press.

Barber, B. R. (2004). *Fear's empire: War, terrorism, and democracy.* New York, NY: W. W. Norton.

Barber, B. R. (2012). Can we teach civic engagement and service-learning in a world of privatization, inequity, and interdependence? *Journal of College & Character, 13*(1), 1–10.

Biddix, J. P. (2006). *The power of estudentprotest: A study of electronically enhanced student activism* (Unpublished doctoral dissertation). University of Missouri-St. Louis, St. Louis.

Biddix, J. P. (2010). Relational leadership and technology: A study of activist college women leaders (ACLWs). *Journal About Women in Higher Education, 3*(1), 25–47.

Biddix, J. P., Somers, P. A., & Polman, J. L. (2009). Protest reconsidered: Activism's role as civic engagement educator. *Innovative Higher Education, 34*(3), 133–147.

Billings, M. S., & Terkla, D. G. (2011). Using a structural equation model to describe the infusion of civic engagement in the campus culture. *Journal of General Education, 60*(2), 84–100.

Bryant, A. N., Gayles, J. G., & Davis, H. A. (2011). The relationship between civic behavior and civic values: A conceptual model. *Research in Higher Education, 53*(1), 76–93.

Butin, D. W. (2012). Rethinking the "apprenticeship of liberty": The case for academic programs in community engagement in higher education. *Journal of College & Character, 13*(1), 1–8.

Carnegie Foundation for the Advancement of Teaching. (2006). *Higher education: Civic mission and civic effects.* Stanford, CA: Author.

Chambers, T., & Phelps, C. E. (1993). Student activism as a form of leadership and student development. *NASPA Journal, 31,* 19–29.

Colby, A., Ehrlich, T., Beaumont, E., & Stephens, J. (2003). *Educating citizens: Preparing America's undergraduates for lives of moral and civic responsibility.* San Francisco, CA: Jossey-Bass.

Dey, E. L., & Associates. (2009). *Civic responsibility: What is the campus climate for learning?* Washington, DC: Association of American Colleges and Universities.

Eagan, K., Herrera, F. A., Garibay, J. C., Hurtado, S., & Chang, M. (2011, May). *Academic achievement among STEM aspirants: Why do Black and Latino students earn lower grades than their White and Asian counterparts?* Paper presented at the Association for Institutional Research Forum, Toronto, Canada.

Engle, S., & Ochoa, A. (1988). *Education for democratic citizenship: Decision making in the social studies.* New York, NY: Teachers College Press.

Featherstone, L. (2002). *Students against sweatshops: The making of a movement.* New York, NY: Verso.

Finley, A. (2011). *Civic learning and democratic engagements: A review of the literature on civic engagement in post-secondary education.* Paper prepared for the US Department of Education as part of Contract: ED-OPE-10-C-0078.

Finley, A. (2012). *Making progress? What we know about the achievement of liberal education outcomes.* Washington, DC: Association of American Colleges and Universities.

Garcia, G. A., & Hurtado, S. (2011, April). *Predicting Latina/o STEM Persistence at HSIs and non-HSIs.* Paper presented at the American Educational Research Association Annual Conference, New Orleans, LA.

Goldfinger, J. (2009). Democratic plaza: A campus space for civic engagement. *Innovative Higher Education, 34*(2), 69–77.

Gutmann, A. (1987). *Democratic education.* Princeton, NJ: Princeton University Press.

Hamrick, F. A. (1998). Democratic citizenship and student activism. *Journal of College Student Development, 39*(5), 449–460.

Harper, W. R. (1905). *The trend in higher education.* Chicago, IL: University of Chicago Press.

Hunter, D. E. (1988). Student activism: Growth through rebellion. In K. M. Miser (Ed.), *Student affairs and campus dissent: Reflection of the past and challenge for the future* (pp. 23–40). Washington, DC: National Association of Student Personnel Administrators.

Jacoby, B., & Associates. (2009). *Civic engagement in higher education: Concepts and practices.* San Francisco, CA: Jossey-Bass.

Jacoby, B., & Hollander, E. (2009). Securing the future of civic engagement in higher education. In B. Jacoby (Ed.), *Civic engagement in higher education: Concepts and practices* (pp. 227–248). San Francisco, CA: Jossey-Bass.

Keeling, R. P., & Associates. (2004). *Learning reconsidered: A campus-wide focus on the student experience.* Washington, DC: The National Association of Student Personnel Administrators, The American College Personnel Association.

Komives, S. R., Lucas, N., & McMahon, T. R. (2007). *Exploring leadership: For college students who want to make a difference* (2nd ed.). San Francisco, CA: Jossey-Bass.

Kuh, G. D. (2008). *High-impact educational practices: What they are, who has access to them, and why they matter.* Washington, DC: Association of American College and Universities.

Kuh, G. D., Kinzie, J., Schuh, J. H., & Whitt, E. J. (2005). *Student success in college: Creating conditions that matter.* San Francisco, CA: Jossey-Bass.

Lopez, M. H., Levine, P., Both, D., Kiesa, A., Kirby, E., & Marcelo, K. (2006). *The 2006 civic and political health of the nation: A detailed look at how youth participate in politics and communities.* College Park, MD: Center for Information and Research on Civic Learning and Engagement.

McCormick, A. C., & McClenney, K. (2012). Will these trees ever bear fruit? A response to the special issue on student engagement. *The Review of Higher Education, 35*(2), 307–333.

Misa, K., Anderson, J., & Yamamura, E. (2005, November). *The lasting impact of college on young adults' civic and political engagement.* Paper presented at the Association for the Study of Higher Education Annual Conference, Philadelphia, PA.

The National Task Force on Civic Learning and Democratic Engagement. (2012). *A crucible moment: College learning and democracy's future.* Washington, DC: Association of American Colleges and Universities. Retrieved from http://www.aacu.org/civic_learning/crucible/index.cfm

Nishishiba, M., Nelson, H. T., & Shinn, C. W. (2005). Explicating factors that foster civic engagement among students. *Journal of Public Affairs Education, 11*(4), 269–285.

Porter, S. R. (2009, November). *Do college student surveys have any validity?* Paper presented to the meeting of the Association for the Study of Higher Education, Vancouver, Canada. (Reprinted in *The Review of Higher Education, 35*(1), 45–76)

Reason, R. D., Cox, B. E., McIntosh, K., & Terenzini, P. T. (2011, January). *Parsing the first year of college: Findings from a comprehensive study.* Paper presented at the annual meeting of the Association of American Colleges and Universities, San Francisco, CA.

Rhoads, R. A. (1997). Interpreting identity politics: The educational challenge of contemporary student activism. *Journal of College Student Development, 38*, 508–519.

Rhoads, R. A. (1998). Student protest and multicultural reform: Making sense of campus unrest in the 1990s. *Journal of Higher Education, 69*(6), 621–646.

Rhoads, R. A., & Rhoades, G. D. (2005). Graduate employee unionization as symbol of and challenge to the corporatization of U.S. research universities. *Journal of Higher Education, 76*(3), 243–275.

Sax, L. (2000). Citizenship development and the American college student. In T. Ehrlich (Ed.), *Civic responsibility and higher education* (pp. 3–18). Phoenix, AZ: Oryx Press.

Seider, S. (2007). Catalyzing a commitment to community service in emerging adults. *Journal of Adolescent Research, 22*(6), 612–639.

Strayhorn, T. (2005). Democratic education and public universities in America. *Journal of College & Character, 6*(3). doi:10.2202/1940-1639.1422

Tabachnick, B. G., & Fidell, L. S. (2001). *Using multivariate statistics* (4th ed.). Boston, MA: Allyn and Bacon.

J. PATRICK BIDDIX is an associate professor and program coordinator in college student personnel at the University of Tennessee.

This chapter synthesizes the common themes across chapters in this volume and argues that campus activists are an integral part of the higher education landscape.

Understanding and Improving Campus Climates for Activists

Georgianna L. Martin

From the advent of the colonial colleges in the 18th century to the present day, campus activism has consistently been part of the fabric of American higher education. As Christopher J. Broadhurst explained in Chapter 1 of this volume, although the issues that spark action and the methods activists use may have ebbed and flowed over the years, one thing remains the same—campus activism emerges on college and university campuses from a desire to change one's community, nation, and world. In this chapter, I first explore the tension between activism as behavior to manage or "deal with" on college campuses and activism and its related constructs as desirable college outcomes. Next, I synthesize the common themes of this volume and argue that campus activists, historically mislabeled as radicals, are an important and integral part of the higher education landscape. Finally, I offer considerations for higher education professionals and scholars invested in improving campus climates for activists.

Activism as an Outcome of College

Consistently scholars and educators have identified civic mindedness or civic engagement as a desirable outcome of college (Bok, 1990; Colby, Ehrlich, Beaumont, & Stephens, 2003; Harvey & Immerwahr, 1995; Nussbaum, 2002). Hersh and Schneider (2005) argued that educators do students a disservice if they neglect to teach them the importance of responsible social action. More recently, scholars have used the construct of socially responsible leadership to explore college students' social-change-related attitudes and values (e.g., Dugan, 2006a, 2006b; Dugan & Komives, 2010; Martin, 2013). Many studies employing socially responsible leadership as an important college outcome use Tyree's (1998) Socially Responsible Leadership Scale to assess students' (a) self-awareness, (b) congruence of

NEW DIRECTIONS FOR HIGHER EDUCATION, no. 167, Fall 2014 © 2014 Wiley Periodicals, Inc.
Published online in Wiley Online Library (wileyonlinelibrary.com) • DOI: 10.1002/he.20107

behavior with personal values, (c) investment of time and energy in activities deemed important, (d) work with diverse others to accomplish common goals, (e) sense of civic and social responsibility, and (f) desire to make the world a better place. Still other scholars have directly identified social and political activism as a desirable college outcome because of its connection to preparing students for engagement in a democratic society (Hurtado, 2004). Pascarella, Salisbury, Martin, and Blaich (2012), for example, explored the impact of diversity experiences on social and political activism during the first year of college. They found that increased exposure to classroom-related diversity topics and interactions with diverse peers had a positive impact on students' growth in social and political activism as early as the first year of college. Studies such as this not only place social and political activism as a desirable college outcome but also explore the educational and environmental conditions that promote such an educational outcome.

Whether educators use the term social responsibility, civic engagement, civic mindedness, social action, social/political activism, or another similar phrase, the quintessential feature of each of these constructs is a desire to make one's community and world a better place. From that perspective, it is difficult to argue against cultivating positive growth on such outcomes during the college years. Educators, at least in theory, appear to overwhelmingly support efforts to help college students grow along these dimensions. However, student growth along such outcome dimensions is likely to be associated with student activism, on campus and in the larger community. These actions may or may not be viewed as positive or developmentally appropriate behaviors by campus administrators. Depending on the magnitude of the action, some activism may simply be viewed by campus educators as a distraction or nuisance to be managed rather than an educational opportunity or a step toward engaged citizenship for college students. Each chapter in this volume has articulated the important role that student activists play in the higher education landscape. They are an integral part of the spirit of a college campus, and many of them have been actively involved in some of the major social changes in our nation over the last century. As Hamrick (1998) indicated, "students who engage in principled dissent and active protest on campus are participating in a different, yet equally valuable, democratic citizenship experience that is worthy of our attention and appreciation" (p. 450).

Common Threads

In this volume, authors have attempted to provide both historical context and contemporary realities for student activists in higher education. Taken together, this collection of chapters offers educators a unique glimpse into experiences and climate for campus activists. Perhaps the most consistent thread that can be found across the chapters is the simple point that social and political activism is alive and well in American higher education in spite of prevailing misconceptions that activists are legends of a bygone era. Whether they are students who become disgruntled with campus policies or students who work for systemic social change in their community, state, nation, or world, activists are visible. Although some no longer march for their cause in a free-speech zone on campus, they are visible through other group organizing efforts such as on social media outlets. An important lesson educators can extract from this series of chapters on campus activism is the changing methods student activists use to organize and express dissent. Perhaps it is important to note, as Cassie L. Barnhardt did in her chapter, that many student activists operate within traditional confines through following the protocols and policies outlined by their institutions of higher education. As Barnhardt indicated, "students worked from their insider status as members of the campus community to seek change" (Chapter 4, p. 53). Although student activists in this century may have shifted tactics from those involved in the social movements of the 1960s and other decades, student activists remain present and visible in higher education.

Another theme present in many of the chapters is the potential for learning that occurs with individuals engaged in social and political activism. As J. Patrick Biddix discussed, his research found that participation in activism through demonstrations was positively associated with "students' value of political and social involvement, making the case for dissent as a means of fostering the development of civically minded" college students (Chapter 6, p. 82). Put another way, acts such as protests, vigils, teach-ins, and other demonstrations appear to aid students in developing what many consider an important outcome of college. Further, Adrianna Kezar and Dan Maxey highlighted the role of collective action in contributing to students' learning of key skills such as strategizing, political savvy, critical consciousness, and mediation. Still other chapter authors mentioned students reporting a sense of responsibility around an issue or a desire to make their campus better than they found it. It becomes clear that the learning that occurs from student engagement in activism is perhaps more than the sum of its parts. Put another way, the knowledge, skills, and attitudes student activists receive or acquire in working toward institutional or social change are more complex than what can be measured in a simple test of skill or list of actions. The passion with which many student activists lean into life will follow them well beyond their college years; how their actions are met in higher education will likely influence the course their future endeavors take.

A final but crucial theme these chapters evoke is the power of the individual in campus activism. As Penny A. Pasque and Juanita Gamez Vargas eloquently remind educators, it is important to remember the "small stories" (Chapter 5, p. 68). Educators who approach campus activists without considering the individual stories—both triumphs and disappointments—do a disservice to the students they purport to serve. Student activists not only reflect a larger movement but individually they also reflect a personal story or experience that has led them to be passionate about the issue they champion. We must remember this small but significant fact about the student activists learning on our college campuses.

Considerations for Campus Professionals

In this section, I discuss a few key considerations for campus professionals interested in cultivating an inclusive climate for student activists. College and university administrators ought to welcome student activism on campus not only through the institution's mission, values, and culture but also through verbal encouragement. Such messages show support for the inclusion of student voice in decision making and the importance of democratic dialogue (Broadhurst & Martin, 2014).

Although some campus professionals may view activists' behaviors as acts to be managed and minimized, perhaps turning to student activists themselves to assist educators in redefining what activism looks like on campus might assist professionals in rewriting the script around student activists in higher education. For example, educators might call on student activists to assist institutional administration in operationalizing what desirable college outcomes such as social action, civic engagement, and social responsibility might look like on their campus.

Multiple chapters in this volume highlight the importance of creating a safe space for student activists on campus. As Strange and Banning (2001) indicated, a sense of community will not likely be experienced in the absence of a sense of safety, inclusion, and involvement on the college campus. Perhaps professionals should consider working with college students to define and envision what a safe and inclusive campus climate might look like for student activists. Similarly, educators might consider the important role that a network of belonging has to students' well-being and overall success in college (Parks, 2000). Intentionally creating a space and structure where student activists can meet one another, engage in constructive dialogue, and find support from campus faculty and staff members might help student activists begin to cultivate a sense of belonging in the collegiate environment.

In their recent portrait of today's student demographic, Levine and Dean (2012) presented the complexity of college students and the values, attitudes, and behaviors they bring with them to campus. They noted that this generation places a high importance on community service and volunteerism and has increased their civic engagement over previous generations.

The current generation of college students thinks globally and acts locally, but as Levine and Dean discuss, they do not have a real knowledge or understanding of the larger world around them. This indictment of the overall portrait of today's college students might suggest to educators that a little social activism might be just what many students need to "cement connections in a world in which our differences increasingly overshadow our commonalities. This has been essential in every generation but it is mandatory for citizenship in the twenty-first century" (Levine & Dean, 2012, p. 185).

If colleges and universities are invested in cultivating social responsibility and civic mindedness among students, then a transformation of institutional culture is needed (Hersh & Schneider, 2005). This shift in culture is one in which all members of an institution—faculty, administrators, student affairs professionals, students, and even alumni—are committed to change. The varying stakeholders within higher education must better understand campus activists who, as individuals often on the forefront of societal changes, engage in activities that help determine the future direction of American higher education.

References

Bok, D. C. (1990). *Universities and the future of America.* Durham, NC: Duke University Press.

Broadhurst, C., & Martin, G. L. (2014). Part of the "Establishment"? Understanding campus climates for student activists. *Journal of College and Character*, 15(2), 75–85.

Colby, A., Ehrlich, T., Beaumont, E., & Stephens, J. (2003). *Educating citizens: Preparing America's undergraduates for lives of moral and civic responsibility.* San Francisco, CA: Jossey-Bass.

Dugan, J. P. (2006a). Explorations using the social change model: Leadership development among college men and women. *Journal of College Student Development*, 47(2), 217–225. doi:10.1353/csd.2006.0015

Dugan, J. P. (2006b). Involvement and leadership: A descriptive analysis of socially responsible leadership. *Journal of College Student Development*, 47(3), 335–343. doi:10.1353/csd.2006.0028

Dugan, J. P., & Komives, S. R. (2010). Influences on college students' capacities for socially responsible leadership. *Journal of College Student Development*, 51(5), 525–549. doi:10.1353/csd.2010.0009

Hamrick, F. A. (1998). Democratic citizenship and student activism. *Journal of College Student Development*, 39(5), 449–459.

Harvey, J., & Immerwahr, J. (1995). *Goodwill and growing worry: Public perceptions of American higher education.* Washington, DC: American Council on Education.

Hersh, R. H., & Schneider, C. G. (2005). Fostering personal & social responsibility on college and university campuses. *Liberal Education*, 91(3), 6–13.

Hurtado, S. (2004). *Preparing college students for a diverse democracy: Final report to the U.S. Department of Education, Office of Educational Research and Improvement, Field Initiated Studies Program.* Ann Arbor: University of Michigan.

Levine, A., & Dean, D. R. (2012). *Generation on a tightrope: A portrait of today's college student.* San Francisco, CA: Jossey-Bass.

Martin, G. L. (2013). The impact of interaction with student affairs professionals on socially responsible leadership development in the first year of college. *Journal of College and Character*, 14(4), 289–299.

Nussbaum, M. (2002). Education for citizenship in an era of global connection. *Studies in Philosophy and Education*, 77(4), 289–303.

Parks, S. D. (2000). *Big questions worthy dreams: Mentoring young adults in their search for meaning, purpose, and faith.* San Francisco, CA: Jossey-Bass.

Pascarella, E. T., Salisbury, M. H., Martin, G. L., & Blaich, C. (2012). Some complexities in the effects of diversity experiences on orientation toward social/political activism and political views in the first year of college. *The Journal of Higher Education, 84,* 467–496.

Strange, C. C., & Banning, J. (2001). *Educating by design: Creating campus environments that work.* San Francisco, CA: Jossey-Bass.

Tyree, T. (1998). *Designing an instrument to measure socially responsible leadership using the social change model of leadership development* (Unpublished doctoral dissertation). University of Maryland, College Park.

GEORGIANNA L. MARTIN *is an assistant professor of higher education and student affairs administration at the University of Southern Mississippi. She also serves as codirector of the Research Initiative on Social Justice in Education (RISE).*

Index

ORDER FORM SUBSCRIPTION AND SINGLE ISSUES

DISCOUNTED BACK ISSUES:

Use this form to receive 20% off all back issues of *New Directions for Higher Education*.
All single issues priced at **$23.20** (normally $29.00)

TITLE	ISSUE NO.	ISBN

Call 888-378-2537 or see mailing instructions below. When calling, mention the promotional code JBNND to receive your discount. For a complete list of issues, please visit www.josseybass.com/go/ndhe

SUBSCRIPTIONS: (1 YEAR, 4 ISSUES)

☐ New Order   ☐ Renewal

U.S.	☐ Individual: $89	☐ Institutional: $311
CANADA/MEXICO	☐ Individual: $89	☐ Institutional: $351
ALL OTHERS	☐ Individual: $113	☐ Institutional: $385

Call 888-378-2537 or see mailing and pricing instructions below.
Online subscriptions are available at www.onlinelibrary.wiley.com

ORDER TOTALS:

Issue / Subscription Amount: $ _____

Shipping Amount: $ _____
(for single issues only – subscription prices include shipping)

Total Amount: $ _____

SHIPPING CHARGES:

First Item $6.00
Each Add'l Item $2.00

(No sales tax for U.S. subscriptions. Canadian residents, add GST for subscription orders. Individual rate subscriptions must be paid by personal check or credit card. Individual rate subscriptions may not be resold as library copies.)

BILLING & SHIPPING INFORMATION:

☐ **PAYMENT ENCLOSED:** *(U.S. check or money order only. All payments must be in U.S. dollars.)*

☐ **CREDIT CARD:** ☐ VISA ☐ MC ☐ AMEX

Card number _____Exp. Date_____

Card Holder Name_____Card Issue # _____

Signature _____Day Phone_____

☐ **BILL ME:** *(U.S. institutional orders only. Purchase order required.)*

Purchase order # _____
Federal Tax ID 13559302 • GST 89102-8052

Name_____

Address_____

Phone_____ E-mail_____

Copy or detach page and send to: **John Wiley & Sons, One Montgomery Street, Suite 1200, San Francisco, CA 94104-4594**

Order Form can also be faxed to: **888-481-2665**

PROMO JBNND